Contents

List of Plates

Chapter 1
Preliminaries

A spectacular increase of public interest in the archaeological field has arisen; books have sprung up almost like mushrooms in recent years, and the majority sell briskly. Popular magazines and Sunday newspaper supplements print widely read articles on the subject, many illustrated with attractive photographs either of objects found or of the dig itself. 'Dig-It-Yourself' archaeology clubs have been organized for amateurs, and the result of such widespread attention has, in turn, stimulated professionals to assess the value of publicity relative to their particular projects, and depend more than ever upon the photographer.

Anybody who knows anything at all about archaeology has heard the familiar phrase, 'to dig is to destroy'. The best method yet devised for saving what is destroyed is archaeological photography – to make permanent on film the total efforts of an excavation, efforts which otherwise can be recorded only by words or drawings, both not fully adequate alone. The camera, in the hands of a skilled archaeological photographer, preserves a record of destruction that is a necessary function of any excavation. Naturally not everything found need be put on film, as many objects fail to contribute something distinctly significant towards the record. Therefore much of the photographer's efforts and skills, to say nothing of time, will be directed to differentiating the more from the less important.

While objectives of archaeological photography have remained quite unchanged since its inception, techniques of achieving these aims have been in a state of sweeping modification, brought about not only by remarkable improvements in cameras and films, but also by modern transportation, communication, and availability of items and conveniences which a few short years ago would have been considered impossible of achieving – or at least a long time distant. Ever since the only book in the field was published,[1] so many technical and philosophic advances in equipment and theory have occurred to alter methods that a photographer accustomed to more traditional practices may now find much difficulty in accepting the newer ones, partly because of the skepticism, no doubt, that invariably attends the new and partly because it is easier to do things the way they have always been done. And

certainly there are even more far-reaching transformations in the offing for the near future which undoubtedly will make recent ones appear insignificant by contrast.

A distinction perhaps worth noting here is that there are two varieties of photographers found at a site: 1. photographers who may be also archaeologists and 2. archaeologists who may be also photographers. Alison Frantz made this observation clear when she said 'although the number of excavation photographers is small, few archaeologists can escape the necessity, at one time or another, of taking pictures of vases, inscriptions, or statues in small provincial museums, or sometimes even of holes in the ground.[2] Miss Frantz went on to note[3] that without special training they must do work of a most exacting kind, usually without being able to return for a retake when the first photograph proves unsatisfactory, and thus a lack of training is a misfortune.

Archaeology and photography have grown up together. As techniques in the former have developed, more and better photography has been demanded; and better photography has contributed to improved archaeology. Today the photographer is as vital a part of any archaeological team as any other member, and his is a full-time job at a site of even fair size, the task including, besides the making of pictures in the field and developing and printing them, also the copying of plans and drawings and the studio photography of objects found, particularly if the latter are not to be removed from the country where discovered.

In the early years of scientific archaeology photographers were more or less merely tolerated as a kind of necessary evil; and they were always accused of getting in the way, holding up progress in the dig to get a shot, or demanding much sweeping and cleaning of the site for their pictures. Fortunately this attitude has changed rather completely, the value of photographers having been fully demonstrated over the years as knowledgeable and competent members of the team, and as directors have discovered what good photography could mean, especially when it came to writing reports, lecturing, and publishing results of the expedition. At home base many a member of the team has needed to refer to photographs for details overlooked or not entered in the site journal. Actually the complete success of the expedition may, to a large degree, ultimately depend upon the photographic record. Though both good and proper equipment are required, nevertheless it is the photographer who must use it correctly and with artistry.

Despite the fact that the photographer's place is important to the expedition, he is a specialist, as indeed are most members of the team;

and there can develop some formidable obstacles as a result. Carlton Coon has said that 'mound-digging archaeologists are divided into excavators, architects, experts, and the like. Their most difficult problem in the field is keeping out of one another's hair.'[4] There are other dilemmas too, and these will be examined in due course.

Formerly the photographer had to do much direction of sweeping and preparing the check strips, sections, and other areas to be photographed, but now experienced site directors are well versed in these requirements – at a considerable saving of valuable time to the photographer, who then can devote more of his efforts to other practical aspects of his assignment.

The first requisite of an archaeological photographer is that he thoroughly knows photography – a self-evident requirement. Next he must be entirely familiar with what archaeology is, what it attempts, and how it is done – an awareness of the intrinsic values of the field coupled with a scientific attitude that heeds the many inevitable details necessary to the successful accomplishment of the task. Without the foregoing fundamentals in archaeology, a photographer would literally have to be led by the hand – have to be told in nearly every instance what pictures should be taken and what effects or points to try and emphasize; and few people, who are not photographers of some skill themselves, can properly so direct a photographer in achieving the best results. Skill in photography is never a substitute for knowledge in archaeology – or vice versa. However, this situation is probably unrealistic, since no expedition leader would dare chance to sign on a photographer were he not convinced that the latter had considerable knowledge of archaeology – at least theoretically if not through firsthand experience.

ARTISTRY OR TRUTH

In nearly every case where photography is a necessary adjunct to some other field, the question invariably arises as to whether or not it is possible that photographic results can be artistic (in the aesthetic sense), or do the more technical aspects create requirements prohibiting this approach? While artisty may not be paramount, there are certain things that can be done which are considered in the realm of aesthetics, things like leading lines, balance, center of interest, and so forth, principles that perhaps can be used more readily in general views than specific ones,

3

except even in the latter it may be surprising to some persons just how much the principles also can be applied. There should be a determined effort consciously to use aesthetic principles without willfully sacrificing any informational aspects. With filters, as an example, tone areas can be varied for contrast and skies can be darkened for dramatic effects, to mention just two of several artistic modifications possible.

It has been said by many people, photographers and otherwise, that the camera is an awful liar. It can deceive the eye unmercifully at times, for it not only stretches the truth with optical illusions, but it often shatters the truth with unknowing tone or color blindness. This occurs particularly with black and white films, less often with color films, though the latter are not without their faults at this point. Despite the fact that the camera is our most superior invention in visually recording our surroundings, we have learned to be prudently alert, fearful that what it pictures is falsified by its inhumanness. We too easily misinterpret its product with our subjective eyes or minds. Just as a single example of the difference between human and camera vision, two adjacent areas seen readily by the human eyes as being different in color may turn out to be indistinguishable in a black and white print when the proper filter was not used to cover the camera's eye. Therefore a large part of the photographer's concerted efforts will be to try to show the truth as he sees it and not as the camera may see it. One author notes in a similar direction and adds another important observation: 'the cardinal photographic principle to keep in mind is that any photograph taken must clearly indicate *what* is intended to be illustrated. To put it differently, any archaeological photograph should declare at once to the viewer *why* it was taken at all.'[5] The latter point is a highly significant one, and every photographer, regardless of in what photographic field he is working, ought to have it firmly entrenched in his mind.

PURCHASING AND TESTING

It is likely that the necessary camera equipment has been purchased and used in a previous season, and if so the photographer may have to use it, even though the equipment was not of his choosing and possibly not to his liking. Such circumstances could make his work an arduous chore, perhaps ending in less than totally satisfactory results. I do not imply that all present archaeological photographic equipment is worthless, or that it can even be considered undesirable; it may be in fact exactly the

type with which the photographer can work best and might choose if he were to order it. Yet the chances are good that a fair amount of archaeological equipment, if not nearly antique, is at least outmoded. This condition frequently pertains to long-established units where a seemingly ever-present paucity of funds conspires to prevent the purchase of newer equipment, and it is deemed feasible to use it 'just one more year'! Certainly it is possible to get good pictures with old and what may have been at one time standard equipment, for it has been done and is being done; nor should one disparage either such equipment or previous results with it. However, any archaeological photographer is usually hampered with enough handicaps as it is, so that improvements in equipment or methods should be welcome, not only to the photographer but also to the director, both of whom then can be better assured of the required results. Though budgets always appear to be skimpy and smaller than it is reckoned they should be, photography is one department where slighting can be somewhat shortsighted – not that there has to be an extravagant accumulation of photographic paraphernalia, but care should assiduously be taken to provide those items which will get the job accomplished most successfully. If this means ruthlessly ridding the larder of old equipment for the purchase of new, the request should be done without hesitation, else when a photographer regards his present equipment not suitable to the requirements, yet is forced to go along with it, the responsibility is at least partly with the director. Even though a photographer from the previous season is to use the equipment, it is always well – and reasonable – to reassess any continuing components in the light of possible improvement, to say nothing of worn-out items.

Provided it is determined that new equipment would be advantageous and is to be procured, there are several important suggestions that have proved themselves in the past. One, it is often wise to select a single supplier and deal exclusively with him. Naturally he must be unquestionably competent, have integrity, and be able to supply most equipment and materials at a professional discount. Experienced photographers usually have such a dealer with whom they regularly deal and in whom they have confidence, but if the photographer is new to the particular location, he must seek the advice of other professionals about dealers in the immediate area, a reputable supplier having a personal interest in both selling the right equipment and in servicing it if needed.

Two, all newly acquired equipment (and this also applies to that already existing) should be rigorously tested in every possible detail before being packed for shipment to the dig: lenses for definition,

shutters and diaphrams for accuracy, bellows for light leaks, synchro-nization for good contacts, and so on. Professionals seldom ignore this absolute necessity for thorough testing, but in a rush it has happened – sometimes to the detriment of the project; it should never be permitted, because competent repair facilities at any city near the site are probably woefully inadequate or more likely provokingly non-existent, so some or all of the season's work can possibly depend upon careful preliminary checking. At one small site where processing was delayed until return, no useable negatives at all were obtained due to a malfunctioning of the camera's shutter! Even assuming there is a camera repair establishment nearby, shop personnel may be unfamiliar with foreign (to them) makes of equipment, and valuable time undoubtedly will be lost while waiting for the item to be shipped to some distant facility for repair. Unless a second camera was available, progress of the dig could be seriously handicapped.

Three, every possible contingency should be systematically pondered before making a choice of equipment; such things as weather, geography, availability of water, kind of quarters for darkroom, and dozens of other likely stringent conditions will influence a final determination. Expert opinion should be sought from seasoned archaeologists, and of course the director consulted. Extensive research on the known circumstances is necessary when the photographer is new to a dig, even though he may have had extensive experience in similar areas elsewhere. That nothing should be taken for granted is an incontrovertible axiom, since once on location it is usually too late to make any changes, even relatively simple ones.

Four, make a purchase list well in advance, one that includes every large and small item you can reasonably imagine will be needed, and from time to time you will think of other indispensable things to add (see Appendix A, p. 118, for a starting list). Get other people to look at it and offer their suggestions.

Fortunately from the photographic point of view little archaeological activity occurs in areas of extreme cold. Naturally there are some excep-tions, such as remains of Scythians in the Altai Mountains. When there is need to excavate in the colder climates, it has to be accomplished after the ground has thawed, meaning the summer months. So special 'winterizing' of camera equipment is unnecessary (a must for arctic and antarctic explorers, climbers of Mount Everest, etc.), as pictures in colder climates will be taken at the warmer times, both of the year and day. Not so fortunately, however, a major amount of archaeology is

pursued in hot or humid climates – or both, an activity which requires that special precautions be instituted and maintained against dust and heat in hot but dry regions and against humidity and heat in tropic climates where fungi are an ever-present hazard, particularly to films, papers, and lenses.

One general precautionary measure is to have cameras thoroughly cleaned during the winter months by competent servicing (preferably by the original manufacturer) if they were used the previous season in excessively dusty or humid locations.

PACKING

General instructions and a target date for packing will be distributed by the expedition leader (or someone he designates) well in advance. Equipment, films, papers, chemicals, and other items should be ordered in sufficient time to be on hand two weeks or more before this date. In fact things like cameras or strobes should be delivered considerably ahead of this to insure proper testing. There will also be a request from the expedition leader that the number and sizes of boxes required for shipment be furnished by the photographer (similar requests for such information go to all departments). When one knows from past experience what will be needed by way of crates, the problem is slight; but if this is his first venture, the photographer had better get some sage advice.

Actually the first job may well be to determine how much films, papers, and chemicals is necessary, though these take up a relatively slight amount of the total shipping space. An estimate arrived at for films, then paper and chemicals is only a matter of simple mathematics. Experience can again assist and the site director will be of considerable help in appraising the possibilities in the way of the number of pictures that might be needed, but to be safe always order some over and above the original estimate.

Packing lists for each box will be wanted, and these cannot be made out until the boxes are actually packed. However, a preliminary list by type of equipment and materials will greatly facilitate making the final ones. Such a preparatory step will already have been taken by the photographer in arriving at a decision as to exactly what is necessary for the operation. One sensible way of making out such a list is to divide the items into three or more sections: field equipment, darkroom equipment and supplies, studio equipment, and movie or other

specialized items. Final packing lists should be typed in at least five copies for: 1. the expedition leader; 2. the director; 3. the home base (in the event that a case goes missing and items have to be reordered and reshipped); 4. the photographer; and 5. a copy to be packed inside the case.

An objective of good packing is to conserve space resolutely, so every inch of space in a box must be used. No holes of any consequence can be allowed, for such holes are not only wasteful of space but permit the contents to shift with likely disastrous developments. Small holes between cans and bottles should be stuffed with wads of newspaper (plastic rather than glass bottles should be ordered when possible), and these wads should be left in the crates for use upon return. Though powdered chemicals are factory-sealed in tins, it is well to pack them quite separately from films and papers – just as a precaution. Small packages and boxes within should be well labeled. Tripods can have cradles made for them inside the crates and be strapped into them. Cameras should be well padded against bumps that the crates most certainly will sustain.

The boxes furnished will be lined with a waterproof material and be screwed together rather than nailed; and the covers will later be screwed on. Then there may be a metal strapping put around the crate to complete the packing. Much depends upon the customs at the port of entry as to just the exact type of crating. On the outside will probably be the expedition name and code number. Unless otherwise directed, *do not* put on them 'PHOTO EQUIPMENT', thinking this will ensure more gentle handling, as in many countries such a label is an open invitation to thievery. A code number for the purpose will suffice. Any special customs specifications will be known and passed on by the expedition leader. Despite the fact that the outside of the crate may be clearly marked with an arrow and words 'THIS SIDE UP', don't count on it being the position in which the case will travel.

All equipment should be insured against, theft, loss, and damage, the cost being low, since equipment is too hard to come by in archaeological expeditions not to spend a little additional for such protection.

TRAVELING

Responsibilities for pictures may well begin before reaching the site; they may start at home base in the photographing of charts, 'type'

pottery, actual objects in museums for comparison with things which may be found at the dig, and so forth. Photographs of the trip may be wanted for publicity purposes, and other excavations may be visited on the way. All of these opportunities should be anticipated and provided for by having the necessary cameras and films in the photographer's personal possession. It will entail the personal carrying of at least a 35-mm camera and maybe a movie camera and tripod.

Chapter 2
Photography in the Field

Because photographs are so significant a part of the archaeologist's permanent record, they must clearly report the complete progress of the excavation (see Plates 1 and 2). As each layer is uncovered, regardless of what kind of excavation – grid, trench, or otherwise – a step-by-step photographic record is imperative. Good recording will define every part of the site, each section, and all features such as walls, stratification, evidence of destruction and rebuilding, and objects found buried. Roland Robbins says 'it is important to show the area from all angles, picturing the shape and elevation of the site itself, as well as the streams, the vegetation, and the contours of the adjoining countryside; shots from as many points of the compass as possible should be made at a distance of about a hundred yards'.[6] Taking views of the area before it is disturbed is not always feasible, but such panoramas do furnish a more comprehensive record; and at many locations excavation may start with a transit rather than a shovel, so photos must also be taken of this activity. While most of the photographic record will consist of just inanimate areas or objects, some should include field personnel or workmen as a matter of human interest; pictures specifically for public relations particularly need this approach (see Plates 5 and 6). Certainly if a movie is planned, not only people, but people doing things is mandatory.

Perhaps the first big question that needs attention is 'what cameras are required?' Too many variables exist to recommend particular equipment to the exclusion of all else as universally suitable; the equipment hasn't been made that will do every job. And the choice will largely depend upon things like the photographer's experience, location of the dig, length of time to be on location, and a whole host of other potential factors. Added to the foregoing is the variable of the dig's size, a large excavation requiring the 'full treatment', but a small one a minimum of photographic activity. The following pages cover the majority of aspects that may conceivably occur in a major dig, much probably being irrelevant to one of a limited size. Choice of cameras may depend too upon what might ordinarily be considered circumstances not so ordinary, such as a known lack of water for processing, but

Plate 1. General view of ruins at Aphrodisias, archaeological site directed by
Kenin Erim of New York University

Plate 2. Corinthian and Ionic temples with good detail

normally the choice has to do with preference based upon practical experience. And given the same equipment one photographer will do a superb job, while another may turn in a mediocre or even poor one. All that can (and should) be suggested is the many possibilities, advantages and disadvantages, and here and there for a very special reason, the author's personal choice.

CAMERAS

It is advisable and probably necessary to have several cameras at any sizable dig, not only because one kind should not be expected to do all types of work, but also because accidents do happen and/or equipment may become disabled. And, as will be noted later, a camera for close-up work left in the site studio would often save valuable time. Then there may need to be movies taken in addition to stills, and most probably color slides and maybe color prints. The days are gone when an archaeological photographer can tote along one big plate camera and expect to get the whole job accomplished adequately.

There have been at least three major revolutions in photography itself to drastically alter modern archaeological photography: the invention and development of 1. the miniature camera, 2. color films, and 3. the Polaroid process. Each of these and its resulting impact will be discussed later in the appropriate places.

Modern still cameras can be grouped roughly into four categories, though there is some obvious overlapping: 1. view and press cameras, 2. roll film cameras, 3. miniature cameras, and 4. sub-miniature cameras. Each group will now be examined in turn.

VIEW AND PRESS CAMERAS
Cameras using plates of $6\frac{1}{2} \times 8\frac{1}{2}$ in., 8×10 in., or even larger sizes have been the standard work horses of the past for archaeological photographers. They were big, bulky, and cumbersome, needing equally large tripods or supporting stands. Over the past few years there has been a gradual shift toward smaller sizes, so that most of the former giants have been discarded or probably should be. Today a 4×5-in. camera can undoubtedly be used more profitably than any larger size, and some experienced photographers in the field work exclusively and successfully with 35-mm cameras. This shift has not come easily, for

prejudice in archaeological circles against smaller negatives is strong – and not without some reason. The old simple cameras, for instance, had little to go wrong with them (even a shutter was unnecessary), whereas today's smaller cameras, with all of their mechanical complexities, can never hope to be quite so reliable – but washing clothes by hand is more reliable in this sense than with a washing machine, yet we don't do the former by choice any more when we can do the latter.

If a relatively simple camera of fairly good size is desired, the 4 × 5-in view camera may be the answer. Because it is simple it is also less costly than, let us say, a press camera of the same size. Still the negative size (or a print from it) is large enough for viewing without enlargement to determine if the quality and content are what is wanted. Basically a view camera is a movable metal bed (track or bar) with upright frames front and rear (to secure the lens board and film holder) with a bellows between. Numerous adjustments permit complex swings, shifts, tilts, and rises for achieving specialized control of linear distortion, necessary features in most architectural photography and often desirable ones in archaeological photography. These latter features cannot be considered simple, but little can go amiss mechanically with their functions. To the lens board can be attached many different lenses, a variety of wide-angle, normal, or telephoto lenses being readily available. A model with extension bellows, preferably up to 22 in., is desirable for extreme close-ups, except that the use of supplemental lenses is always possible instead of the long extension. Since a view camera has no viewfinder, all focusing and composing must be done on the ground-glass back, which because of its relatively large size, is distinctly an advantage, though it must be pointed out that unless one is used to viewing things reversed and upside down in a camera, the task may be quite onerously difficult. But to the person accustomed to such a procedure, this problem is seldom of great consequence with most archaeological pictures where no movement of subject is involved, the photographer having ample time for focusing and composition. Sheet films of the 4 × 5-in. size are inserted in holders (two pieces of film in each holder; one on each side) and slid into the camera's back in front of the ground-glass. Then the dark slide of the holder is withdrawn for an exposure. Most modern view cameras have what is termed a Graflok-type back, which means that in addition to sheet film holders and packs, accessory holders for magazines, roll films, Polaroid films, and miniature film are available, taking black and white, color, or specialized films. A later section on films will detail this further.

View cameras are made by Linhof, Graflex, Carl Heitz, Calumet, and other reliable concerns. Incidentally there are 5 × 7-in, 8 × 10-in., and even larger view cameras on the market, but with these we get back to the old plate camera of unwieldy dimensions. Some photographers may yet prefer these larger sizes, so it is well to know they are commercially available even now, since they are still used for studio work where the retouching of negatives is needed. Details in archaeological negatives, according to tradition, are never retouched, so large film cameras are not selected for this particular reason, rather for other reasons indicated earlier. One singular advantage of most view cameras over other types, especially for close-ups, is that they can be focused by moving either the front lens board or the rear film holder section, both of which slide along the bed. In common with press cameras, backs can also be rotated from the horizontal to the vertical position, and some cameras can shoot at any degree in a full circle. As can be seen the view camera is a highly versatile yet simple instrument for the field. Its chief disadvantages are: 1. bulkiness (even the 4 × 5-in.) and weight, 2. that one must work rather slowly with it, and 3. the longer focal lengths of its lenses means that a relatively longer exposure is necessary for overall sharpness.

Most of the advantages of the view camera are also incorporated in the best 4 × 5-in. press cameras, with additional benefits of coupled viewfinders and range finders. Except for the Linhof, none now manufactured have swinging backs, a fairly desirable though not indispensable feature. The press camera of course can be hand held if necessary, and can be used with more facility in crowded places and from airplanes (if aerial photography is a possibility). But normally it should, like the view camera, be set upon a rock-steady tripod. Rarely it might be advantageous to use it upside down for extreme downward linear distortion correction, and the press camera can do this with less awkwardness than can the view. Another decided benefit of most press cameras is their compactness and the fact that they fold inside their own cases for added protection. As with the view cameras the press also have the Graflok-type back and will accept the same adapters. The 4 × 5-in. has been the standard size for press photographers for many years, though a 5 × 7-in. also is manufactured.

In more recent years some of the leading firms have developed $2\frac{1}{4} \times 3\frac{1}{4}$-in. press cameras, but here again the Linhof is presently the only one in this size with the full complement of distortion adjustments. Most people will agree that the $2\frac{1}{4} \times 3\frac{1}{4}$-in. negative is still of ample dimensions for visual examination, and the lightness of this camera

coupled with its versatility and its use of less expensive films will undoubtedly see its employment by some photographers in archaeological work, perhaps eventually replacing the 4 × 5-in. The smaller size does not require a monster tripod, and it can be carried about with a minimum of effort. At the moment a drawback compared to the 4 × 5-in. is the fewer types of films available for it, although this may change in the future.

Any 4 × 5-in. press camera or view camera can be used as a substitute for an enlarger with the proper lamp adapter attached to its back, but probably there is no need for such arrangement in an expedition using this size, the original negatives being large enough for contact prints. Press cameras, like the views, also take a wide range of lenses, except that they have to be purchased for the particular cameras, being coupled as they are to the range finders and viewfinders. Ground-glass focusing is also easily done with the press cameras enabling the user to more accurately check depth of field if desired. There are hardly any real disadvantages of importance that accrue to the press cameras, unless of course personal taste runs to a smaller size. But even as far back as 1946, Atkinson was recommending[7] the small reflex cameras of the $2\frac{1}{4}$-in. square size as being excellent for archaeology.

ROLL FILM CAMERAS

These cameras are intermediate in size between the larger sheet film ones and the more diminutive miniatures. As indicated in the previous section the 4 × 5-in. views and all of the major press cameras can be adapted to take rolls, and here we are referring to what is commonly called the 120 film size (some take 828), which in the press cameras is usually a $2\frac{1}{4}$ × $3\frac{1}{4}$-in. format, but in the roll cameras is normally $2\frac{1}{4}$ × $2\frac{1}{4}$ in., a square format. Most roll film cameras are single or twin-lens reflex models, such as the Hasselblad or Bronica (single) or Rolleiflex (twin). The single-lens variety is probably to be preferred for two reasons: 1. they have interchangeable backs so that various films can be used in any order without having to finish the roll; and 2. there is no parallax problem for close-ups (compensating methods of overcoming this last are available for twin-lens cameras if a tripod is used and if there is no movement or action that requires instantaneous viewing). Of the twin-lens reflex cameras, only the Mamiya presently has three or more interchangeable pairs of lenses. The two single-lens reflex cameras mentioned above have interchangeable lenses too. But neither type of reflexes have the swings, tilts, rises, and shifts of the

view or press variety. Furthermore it is extremely doubtful that they could be used satisfactorily without being coupled to an enlarger for prints. Yet this may not in itself be a deciding factor, as certainly the ease with which they can be used is a strong advantage. But whether this single feature outweighs all of the benefits of the larger cameras is something that only the photographer can judge when taking into consideration his previous experience and any special requirements. A definite disadvantage is the possible waste of film for cameras without interchangeable backs, for if only one or two shots are needed at the moment and then the roll has to be developed immediately, the rest goes into the circular file. In practice however this system is not as costly as it sounds, since the price of a 120 roll is not a great deal more than several sheets of the larger films and one may not often need to be so deliberately wasteful.

Though adapters are available for 35-mm color transparencies to fit the backs of view and press cameras, the resulting image is tiny; but with similar adapters on a $2\frac{1}{4}$-in. square reflex with an interchangeable back, there is not this much of a differential, the lenses being of relatively shorter focal length and the image-to-film ratio altered in favor of the smaller film. Therefore a camera of this choice might be good if the photographer wanted to obtain both fair sized black and white negatives and 35-mm color transparencies while using the same camera.

One other possible use of these roll film cameras is in underwater archaeological photography, their smallness being a real asset (see section on Underwater Photography in Chapter 4, p. 88).

MINIATURE CAMERAS

A few years ago archaeologists would have spoofed at the thought of a serious photographer using a miniature as main camera in an excavation. But in recent years it has been done, sometimes with most favorable results. As one might guess its successful use very much depends upon the skill of the photographer and the careful handling and treatment of the film. Even the smallest scratch or pinhole will cause serious difficulties in blow-ups and may make the negative useless, so under often difficult processing conditions, scratches and blemishes or other hazards to enlargement are likely to plague the performance of these small cameras. For all that, if it were not for the smallness of the negative, the miniature camera would probably outstrip in popularity all other cameras at a dig, its convenience and portability allowing the photographer to move quickly from one place to the next, shooting from

many angles and distances in the space of a few minutes and most likely doing it all hand held. No longer need one fear any lack of definition on the small film, as many persons have amply demonstrated that huge table-sized blow-ups are feasible without much appreciable loss of detail. Certainly the resolution is finer than that which a printing press requires for reasonably sized plates. Even as long ago as 1950, Alison Frantz said[8] that the miniature camera is *essential* for identification and records at a dig. Now it can be added that the camera's place is unquestioned, at least as an auxiliary.

True the miniature cameras do not have the full distortion correctives of the larger view or press cameras, but in reality we have become quite accustomed to seeing vertical lines not vertical in newspapers, magazines, and many other places where illustrations in photographic form are used. The making sure that vertical lines are not distorted seems to be less and less of a necessity than once was thought, perhaps because people are becoming more sophisticated to the point where such distortions are more readily accepted. Undoubtedly this has come about from the fact that most persons of any means today own cameras and take pictures, realizing in the process that undistorted verticals in pictures are more the rare exception than the rule. If the phase of archaeological photography involved is to be basically architectural in nature, such as with buildings in Pompeii or a Central American temple, for instance, then undistorted verticals might be desirable; but below ground verticals that slant do not seem to overly disturb the eye of most people. Most persons tend to expect to see such lines at an inclined position because of conditioning – a mental set.

A recent development by Nikon has partly overcome the lack of perspective control by the design of their PC-Nikkor lens that shifts 11 mm off-axis in any of 360°. This lens does, therefore, correct vertical distortions (or distortions in any other single direction). It is, however, a wide-angle lens (35 mm), but focuses from 12 in. to infinity and stops down to f/32.

The short focal lengths of miniature cameras (2 in. is normal) makes possible the use of relatively wide diaphram openings and hence short exposures. Moreover, one could probably take a dozen shots from as many different angles with a miniature in the space of time that one photograph was being taken with a view camera. If roll film cameras are easy to carry around, the miniatures are easier; one can even put a range-finder Leica with a collapsible lens in one's coat pocket with room left over for spare film and a sunshade. Range-finder 35s, like the somewhat

larger roll film cameras, have parallax problems for close-ups. Single-lens reflex miniatures are a bit more bulky than the range finders, but the difference is so little and the advantage of seeing the depth of field being photographed is so great that the size of the former nearly puts them in the same category as the view or press cameras at this point. However, no one will deny that their relatively smaller viewing areas may be more difficult to work with, particularly for persons wearing eyeglasses, though this is perhaps more than compensated for by their extreme depth of field that makes pinpoint focusing often unnecessary. Down in the darkness of a trench the view in many of these cameras is much better (because of their light-gathering prisms) than it is with the view or press type.

The apparent wastage of film when only a few shots are required is even greater than with the roll film cameras. In practice the cost of film is small and the possibility of getting a better picture out of an assortment of twenty moderately rapid shots may be better than spending much time with a larger camera to get one. Also what one may waste in film is at least partly saved in chemicals, and if water is a problem, the small quantity needed for processing miniature rolls is considerably less than for sheet films. Moreover, bulk films can be purchased in rolls and loaded into handy cassettes (usable in some 35s) at a considerable saving, and then only the exposed portions of films can be cut off and developed, or short lengths loaded in the first place. A camera like the Contarex or Contaflex has interchangeable backs, just as with some of the $2\frac{1}{4}$-in. square single-lens reflexes.

With all of the aforementioned advantages it should be no surprise to see the miniature finding increasing use in the field. Of course it is necessary to use an enlarger to show up satisfactorily the features of objects or areas photographed in a black and white print, though enlarging is really very little more work than using a printing frame, especially if a dozen or so pictures are done at a single time. But it must be admitted that one cannot adequately read the 35-mm negatives wet, prints having to be made to check upon details. For producing color transparencies in the 2 × 2-in. size, the camera does a superb job, as its wide apertures often permit a brief exposure for even the slower color films. In many other related art fields 2 × 2-in. transparencies for lecture purposes are slowly taking the place of the older $3\frac{1}{4}$ × $4\frac{1}{4}$-in. lantern slides; this revolution has already almost completely occurred in archaeology. Roland Robbins, well known for his restoration of the Saugus Ironworks near Boston, tells[9] how he shot over 3,000 color

transparencies of the digging with a Kodak Bantam camera. Even for black and white publication prints he used the same transparencies.

If it is known that electricity will be unavailable or undependable at the site, the larger negative that requires only contact printing (or just viewing as is) had better be chosen for black and white pictures, since printing can be done with a printing frame in front of a battery lamp if necessary – either this or use the Polaroid system.

SUB-MINIATURE CAMERAS

Only one specialized use is presently required of the sub-miniature in archaeology, and that not for a permanent record. In excavating Etruscan tombs, this small camera has been employed by Carlo Lerici in a peri-scope-like instrument to photograph interiors before the actual excava-tion is attempted for the purpose of determining if such excavation is worthwhile. By this method he examined 130 graves in a ten-week period and opened the best twenty of them.[10] Otherwise the size of the film (16-mm movie film) is too hard to handle in the field and requires excessive amounts of care in achieving even reasonably fair results.

Not mentioned is the single or half-frame camera (one-half of the 35-mm frame) that is finding increasing use by amateurs. Some day it might conceivably replace the 35-mm and do much that the latter now does, perhaps even in terms of lecture purposes. At present it can probably be regarded as a sub-miniature with all of the attendant problems and difficulties.

MOTION PICTURE CAMERAS

Up to now the majority of professional motion picture work done at an excavation has been by persons not usually directly associated with the expedition team (not counting *ad hoc* staff members who are amateurs). That is to say the university, museum, or other institution or society sponsoring the dig may send along a movie photographer to get a particular story on film for either publicity or teaching purposes (or both), or the photographer may have been sent by some commercial venture, a news medium or otherwise. As early as 1954 the BBC Tele-vision Service programmed a series of 'Buried Treasure' that required much filming on location by a team of expert photographers under the supervision of an archaeologist.[11] But seldom has the archaeological team itself set out with movie camera equipment in hand as a matter of regular procedure.

Sometimes one or more of the expedition's members may bring

cameras of their own to make a personal record of the dig, and these have included movie cameras of both the 16-mm and 8-mm sizes. The latter size is considered strictly in the amateur class mainly because of the smallness of the image that can be satisfactorily projected, though modern 8-mm cameras certainly have all of the 'professional' effects like zooms, dissolves, and so forth, and are capable of producing remarkable results. However, if the film is to be shown for a group of over sixty or so, the 16-mm size is an absolute necessity. Even the super–8-mm is not suitable for the larger audiences. One possible change in this situation is the acceptance of the 9.5-mm size developed in Europe. The image size is practically equal to the present 16-mm, the sprocket holes being single and in the middle of each frame line. Whether it lives or dies depends upon commercial problems. That is, the film would cost nearly as much as 16-mm without the possibility of good sound striping. Since today sound pictures are a must for professional showings, and archaeo-logical pictures are no exception, this calls not only for *good* equipment in at least the 16-mm size at 24 fps, but also *much* equipment. Perhaps the latter is one reason for a paucity of movies in the field, shipping space on archaeological expeditions normally being at a premium. However, the main reason beyond doubt is financial. Sky-high costs act as a kind of suppression control. Sometimes these costs can be overcome by seeking the help of a commercial source in return for certain usage rights (which can be to the credit of the expedition and secondarily serve as a type of publicity agent). Naturally all such arrangements take time, but undoubtedly it could be time well spent. Then there is always the possibility of selling prints of good footage when the movie is shot by the archaeological photographer. Movies for teaching purposes mentioned earlier can be a valuable tool for the training of students in archaeology and art history. To see movies of the actual dig in progress, if they are not falsified by Hollywood styling, can do more to initiate a student into the 'living' aspects of the subject than can thousands of good slides, for often the latter somehow tend to be rather impersonal and a bit removed from reality. Life in the movie film is achieved because a well planned motion picture produces a certain continuity which other picture methods can never hope to duplicate. One excellent short but effective movie may sell the board of directors of a foundation on financing a future expedition in a manner no other means could, a potentiality not to be taken lightly.

It may be well to remind the reader that sound can be added at a later date – at home base after the film has been processed, a small

portable tape recorder being employed separately to pick up a few authentic sounds on location to be dubbed on the film after editing. Therefore complicated and expensive synchronized sound equipment could be dispensed with in the field, for this equipment does require batteries and considerable care in maintenance.

Motion pictures necessitate quite different techniques of photography than do stills, and one photographer may not be able, either by experience or time, to handle both; the result, if he tries, being only a mediocre job at each. In large expeditions two photographers therefore might be employed, or some other staff member might be experienced enough with photography to at least assist in more than just carrying equipment.

Unless financed by an independent source, 35-mm movies are undoubtedly out of the question – at least for color – and black and white movies are largely a thing of the past (except for TV, and that's changing rapidly). The cost of film and processing in the large size would be much too expensive in color in proportion to the practical need, the 16-mm size being adequate for nearly all purposes today, as it can be enlarged to the 35-mm size during the printing of copies. A reflex camera, such as Bolex, is recommended though not required.

CAMERA CASES

All cameras used at the site will need cases – without exception – either individual cases or larger compartmented ones. Necessarily the cases will be dependant upon the size of the cameras and how they will be used. The larger view and press cameras will seldom need separate or individual cases; rather they will probably be kept in larger carrying cases of the Graflex fiber-type along with extra lenses, filters, and film holders. Roll film cameras may or may not require such cases; they may be in their individual cases with shoulder straps, especially if they are used as auxiliary cameras or, if main cameras, they may also require a larger supplemental case to hold accessories. The miniature cameras will almost invariably be carried in their own cases, whether primary or secondary in use, and supplemental cases to hold an array of lenses, filters, films, and possibly a second body. The movie camera will be kept, as the larger still cameras, in a case with additional paraphernalia.

Whatever case or cases are put into service they need to be as dustproof and rugged as possible. Excavations seem to be the dustiest places on the face of the earth, and only one particle of it can do inestimable

damage to mechanical parts, to sliding surfaces of film holders, and to surfaces of lenses and filters. In such places the photographer must wage a constant battle against the dust, some of it being so fine as to penetrate the barest hairline of a crack. Plastic bags are invaluable as both dust discouragers and against water accidents and dampness. Dust such as is found in the Middle East, for instance, is a condition which one must experience firsthand to realize its destructiveness. If a small camera is carried in a case with a shoulder strap, there is less of a tendency to set it down temporarily – which frequently may mean on dirt or sand. In humid climates cases must additionally be moisture-proof – at least this is true for those cases in which the camera is to be kept for more than a day's shooting. Leather cases in the tropics are subject to mildew in short order, and thus need to be kept dry and clean of perspiration.

And while the photographer is getting his vantage point chosen, focusing the camera, or waiting for the next picture opportunity, the camera and the case (in which may be kept additional films) can become literally ovens as they sit in the sun – even in relatively high and cool altitudes. Both must be protected in some manner, the case put in the shade, perhaps in a trench or behind a wheelbarrow, while the camera, if a big one on a tripod, might have the focusing cloth or other similar material draped over it for short periods.

LENSES

Newer optics will have both diaphrams and shutters, but older lenses may not include the latter and thereby require long exposures with the lens cap as a substitute. Almost all of the new lenses are synchronized for flash and strobe – an important consideration today – and they should be anastigmatic and color-corrected, for if color is not used at the moment, sooner or later it will be desired, probably sooner.

The archaeological photographer should have at least three lenses for his main camera: 1. wide-angle (short focal length); 2. normal; and 3. telephoto or long focal length, the latter kinds useful for certain restricted purposes such as details of sculpture, inscriptions high upon a cliff face, and other items that would be too distant or distorted with shorter lenses.

Advantages of a short focal length lens are mainly its tremendous depth of field and wide coverage, an absolute must in cramped places.

However, it does have the disadvantages of linear distortion (flattening the field or slanting the verticals above and below eye level) that results from shooting too close to the subject, and the possibility of not covering the corners of large negatives with equal sharpness as the center. This last is another matter for critical checking at home base, and usually applies to only the 4 × 5-in. or larger cameras.

A long lens tends to eliminate linear distortion, since the camera is held or positioned more horizontally in actual use rather than tilted up or down at a decided angle. Its shallow depth of field, by contrast to shorter lenses, could be considered a handicap and may require longer exposures.

Focal lengths (in millimeters) of the usual lenses for various size cameras is found in the accompanying chart (see fig. 1). With any given negative size the focal length of the lens determines the angle of view. For a normal view this length approximates the diagonal dimension of the film and is about 45°. With a wide-angle lens the image is reduced; with a telephoto lens it is increased. The longer the focal length, the longer the extension necessary for close-ups. And the bigger the film size, the longer focal length of lens is needed – with accompanying bulkiness and weight (and expense).

Figure 1. Focal lengths (in millimeters) of lenses according to size of camera

Camera size	Wide-angle	Normal	Telephoto
8 × 10 in.	165	300–60	500
5 × 7 in.	120	210–40	360
4 × 5 in. view	90	150–200	240–70
4 × 5 in. press	90	135–50	240–70
3¼ × 4¼ in.	90	135–50	240–70
2¼ × 3¼ in.	65	100–5	180–240
2¼ × 2¼ in.	65	75–90	180–240
35 mm	35	50–8	90–400+

New lenses come with cases, and these can usually be integrated into a larger carrying case. For old lenses some kind of protective covering will be needed, perhaps improvised, but larger camera stores often have a variety of used cases at very reasonable prices. A lens brush and lens papers should be kept handy for occasional cleaning of the optics, though extreme care must be exercised in sandy and dusty areas about wiping

the surface of the lenses. It is well to know that a skylight filter, which does not materially change the color balance, can serve as a protective shield against blowing sand, dust, or salt water. Some photographers keep such a filter on the camera at all times when in dusty areas or by the sea.

Portrait lenses for close-up photography are of distinct value, especially for the 35-mm reflex camera (Kodak calls them Portra Lenses). Easier to use than bellows when one is taking general views as well, they merely fit over the front lens like a filter. Even with a larger camera, the photographer may choose to use them instead of having to compute the additional exposure necessary when the lens is extended by a bellows. These lenses, as filters, come in standard diameter sizes; they also come in a variety of strengths (diopters), the most useful being +1, +2, and +3. Incidentally the +1 can also be used to create a slight wide-angle effect with a camera that has retracting bellows, such as a view or press camera. Used on the camera, these supplemental lenses are put closest to the camera's lens, and any filters added in front; and if two plus lenses are needed, the stronger is put nearer the camera lens. A −1 lens can be used where bellows can be extended for a slight telephoto effect. Though the optical quality of these lenses may be questioned by a few photographers, when the diaphram is stopped down to a relatively small opening, no really significant deterioration of the image occurs.

Individual cases for these additional optics are available, but combination cases to hold the larger sizes seem hard to come by, so here you may also have to improvise a case. For example, four lenses in the Series VI size fit nicely into the little black tin cans in which Kodak 8-mm movie films are packaged, and a dealer will invariably have some things like this cluttering up his drawers. Such cases take up only a small space – can be carried in the corner of a pocket or a larger bag. But the plus lenses at any rate should have cases, for, although relatively inexpensive, dust can just as easily damage their surfaces as it can that of the camera lenses.

FOCUSING

Sharpness of focus in a photo is a principle requisite to displaying detail, this being true of pictures taken at hundreds of yards or at several inches. In the old days this meant stopping down the diaphram to its smallest opening – to f/.36 or f/.45 – with exposures of six or more minutes. But

many photographers found out by trial and error that all lenses, particularly the older ones, could not be stopped down to their maximum openings and still maintain the best resolution. The optimum focus of such lenses was at some point short of the smallest f/stop. This is seldom the case with modern lenses, which are engineered not to reach this point; therefore the photographer with a recently purchased lens need have little fear in this regard, but here is just one more important reason for a thorough testing of equipment before taking it to the site.

Nevertheless stopping even modern lenses down to their smallest opening may cause at least a slight diffraction of light as the light waves pass by the edges of the diaphram blades. With a small aperture the proportion of rays so deflected is concentrated in a very small area.

Generally speaking the closer the subject is to the camera the more the lens will need to be stopped down (unless a flat surface is being photographed). On the smaller cameras the stopping down action is often automatic, a mechanism closing the diaphram to a pre-set diameter just a fraction of a second before the shutter opens (though a previewing device allows checking the depth of field). It is advisable to use the longest focus lens that the conditions and subject will permit, an aid in distortion control known but sometimes forgotten by professionals.

When a view or press camera is employed, focusing is done under a black focusing cloth, hopefully of rather generous proportions. Experience has proved that a spring clip to fasten the cloth to the front of the camera is a boon in several ways, notably in a stiff wind. And with such a clip in place one does not have to continually retrieve from the ground or from the bottom of a trench the cloth which provokingly has slipped off the camera.

For archaeological photography of buildings at or above ground level, a camera with a rising front is desired by many workers, the principle need being to eliminate empty foreground and include higher portions of a structure without tilting the film plane away from the perpendicular and thus avoid leaning verticals. This could apply also to trenches whose interior space is so confining that tilting the camera cannot be otherwise avoided. If the foregoing principle is to be used for trenches when the camera is positioned on ground level above, the camera would need to be inverted on the tripod, the rising front becoming a falling one. Here is where the press camera has the advantage over the view variety, the latter being more clumsy and difficult to handle upside down. After all, cameras weren't really made to be used in this fashion. To reduce

vertical distortions without turning the camera upside down, the camera could be set on the edge of the check strip, an arrangement that obviates the usual tripod, so a steady support would have to be devised. In this instance a cable release is invaluable during lengthy exposures. To a small degree by dropping the camera's bed (if a press type), the lens board is lowered sufficiently to correct minor vertical distortions (this is a built-in adjustment for wide-angle lenses). In addition to vertical distortion there may be horizontal distortion when the camera takes in an angle shot of a wall so that, let us say, the left portion of the wall is closer to the camera than the right part. Without correction the left area would appear overly large, but this condition can be modified if the camera has a shifting and swinging front like the press or view variety.

For general views the wide-angle lens is frequently required to enable the photographer to stay relatively close and thus see more ground area, for the farther one backs up the flatter and more compressed from front to rear the horizontal depth dimension will appear – unless a higher vantage point can be found back still farther, in which case the normal or even the telephoto lens can be brought into action.

TRIPODS AND LEVELS

An unsteady tripod is almost worse than none at all. With but a few exceptions the heavier the tripod the more stable it is; yet with newer metal alloys some remarkably light but steady tripods are on the market. This being one item that gets much potentially injurious abuse, it must be rugged, capable of absorbing rough treatment without splintering and swelling (if part wood) or bending and breaking (if metal). The telescopic variety may develop sticking troubles, particularly if the legs or sleeves become dented, but there are some types that are extensible without a tight sleeve-like kind of telescopic leg arrangement. Powdered graphite as a lubricant is recommended. Naturally the size of the tripod should be relative to that of the camera, although it is better to have a big tripod supporting a small camera than vice versa.

Probably there should be three tripods available, possibly a fourth if movies are to be taken. There needs to be the main field tripod; and, like the advisability of a separate studio camera, a studio tripod. Then a smaller but steady tripod can be useful for roll or miniature cameras, especially for those sometimes needed jaunts to a nearby museum or

another dig where it is too inconvenient or the distance is too great to consider carrying a larger tripod. All of the tripods should possess sizable and smoothly working pan heads that tilt in two directions (such as the Tiltall) and a center elevating post, the latter an important time saver. For heavy cameras a universal socket-type tripod head is out of the question, but for a smaller camera this attachment is feasible and handy. Since much photography will very frequently be done on uneven ground, at intervals straddling a pile of earth, care in selecting tripods whose braces for legs (if any) will not be too low; under no circumstances should the tripod have wheels. When there are no leg braces at all to keep them from spreading too far apart, with the possibility of dumping the camera to the ground, suitable substitutes can be simply and easily improvised with several lengths of a chain or string (see fig. 2).

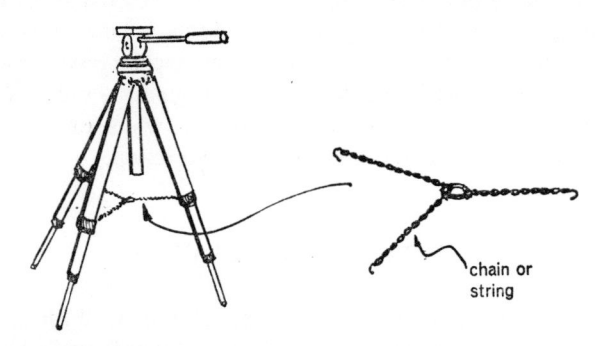

Figure 2.   Improvised braces for tripod legs

Keeping the camera level horizontally with the horizon is a must. Assisting in this can be a bubble level, preferably a directional one, although many of the more expensive tripods often have a circular bubble level built into them. Tripods designed for movies have this arrangement so that panning will be on a level. Where the horizon line is seen in the camera's viewer, leveling is no problem, but when the camera is tilted downward, the leveling device is an easy solution. A directional bubble level can be held along a horizontal surface of the camera and the latter shifted as needed (a circular type will not work for this). A separate small line level 3 or 4 in. in length could readily fit into the pocket or carrying bag, or a small case be made or found for it to hang on the belt. Such levels are readily obtainable at surplus outlets and usually at large hardware stores.

Plate 3. Well-cleaned excavation with different layers of various temples visible

Plate 4. Excellently cleaned areas with sharp edges and brushed stones

THE PHOTO TOWER

It would be the dubious exception rather than the rule that high-angle pictures into a trench would not be advantageous, so at the beginning a portable tower or platform ought to be built, such a structure being useful in addition for the more panoramic views. Natural elevations like trees or hills may in some instances be present from which to get such shots, but the chances are not good that Lady Luck will smile on you very frequently, and the construction of a tower perhaps twelve or fifteen feet in height becomes desirable. This tower has to be sturdy enough to permit vibrationless time exposures and also light enough to carry from one area to another without too much difficulty. Local materials will be the usual answer (except in desert areas), but consideration might be given to shipping some metal scaffolding, or at the least an aluminum stepladder. However, a stepladder is quite unstable on rough ground, because of the minimum distance between its legs. As an expedient it may be possible to improvise a tripod consisting of two poles and a ladder, a precarious perch, but a perch nevertheless from which pictures not requiring a time exposure can be taken (see fig. 3), though a lengthy string controlling the shutter from the ground

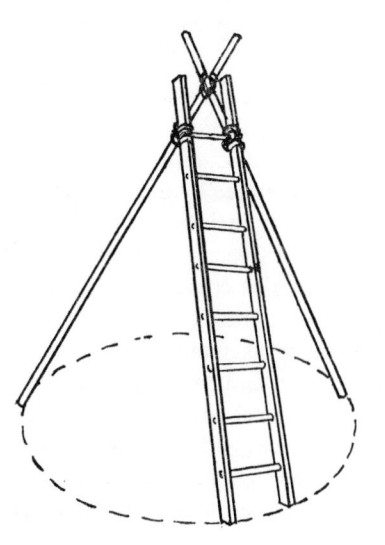

Figure 3. Improvised photo tower
Note: the top rung of the ladder hooks over the tops of the two poles and all are firmly lashed together.

could offer a method of time exposure. Pneumatic devices are also available (used mostly for nature photography) for tripping the shutter from a distance of twenty or more feet from the camera. But a word of caution: more than one photographer has toppled from a tower into a trench or other hole, camera and all, so that the qualities of a suitable stand should be examined with considerable foresight rather than hindsight!

On a small dig the need may not be great enough to spend time or money in the construction of a tower. On the other hand, with large or even small excavations, there is usually a station wagon around, whose roof provides a steady though low perch for pictures.

Possibly at some future date the fully equipped photographer will have available as standard equipment either a helicopter or a bucket seat crane, the kind used for servicing telephone wires high in the air. Such perches would not only produce wonderful high-angle stills, but great movie shots would be feasible. As a matter of fact such a rig has been used upon at least one occasion in the past for archaeological photography on the island of Malta, in the shape of an electric company's lorry.[12]

LIGHT METERS

Two basic types of light meters are available – and necessary. One type measures reflected light, some standard meters of this kind being General Electric, Weston, and Gossin Lunasix (a more sensitive cell is the cadmium sulphide (CdS) powered by mercury batteries rather than the older selenium cell); and the incident-type, two good ones being the Norwood Director and the Spectra 'Combi-500'. Many of the more expensive meters on the market convert to the opposite type, but never quite satisfactorily so. Significantly some of the newer meters are so sensitive that reading can be taken in moonlight with no difficulty. Most have a high and low range, and many have a needle lock. Nearly all modern meters have additional scales for motion picture speeds and Polaroid Land settings as well as the usual ones for conventional still cameras. In fact direct readings for many speeds can be read on the Spectra by the insertion of perforated shields or baffles which come with the unit.

The reflection-type meter best measures flat surfaces and directional light, while the incident-type does a better job for round objects and

non-directional light (or light from several directions). The archaeological photographer will encounter both of these situations, so both meters are recommended. As a matter of fact this is one department that might have two of each, for exposure accuracy is vital, else the film supply will be depleted by errors, perhaps exhausted. If the film is not to be developed on location because of no water or other reasons, accurate meters are essential. An accessory for the Spectra is the G.G. Photoreader, an adapter allowing the taking of direct readings off the ground-glass of the camera – quite a worthwhile item.

ILLUMINATION

One of the most difficult things on the site with which a photographer must work is lighting. Without proper illumination pictures usually might just as well not be taken at all, for they may not show either what is wanted or what is really there. After all, light is the basis of photography. Consequently the photographer has to be aware of what light does in a photo, how to use it to advantage, and to be persistent in watching for the best light conditions. Assisting mightily in the latter is a temporary notebook into which he can jot down lighting conditions at a certain spot at different times of the day for the purpose of finding which angle of the sun shows an area or object *in situ* to the best effect – or perhaps a sunless day is the quality of light needed to accomplish the desired results.

Shadows plague the archaeological photographer's life. For example, one part of a trench may be in deep shadow while another part is in bright sunlight, resulting in a contrast between them that is too great for the film's latitude to properly record the detail in each area – and the latitudes of color films are far less than those for most black and white materials (see Plate 3). More than a few photographers have operated on the principle that pictures should *never* be taken in full sunlight, but this seems too rigid a stand, as will be noted in some of the following procedures. In a few locations where a dig is in progress, the sun never ceases to shine during the day, clouds being almost never present to screen it, so, failing a sunless condition, a tarp held by workmen to cast a shadow (if the area to be photographed is small enough) is helpful, or if this is not feasible, making use of the early morning light ('first light' as it is sometimes called) can achieve similar results, although only at the expense of a tremendous increase in exposure. The latter is no

solution whatsoever with color films, however, for early morning light almost invariably produces a bluish balance that renders colors untrue. And even at midday objects in shadow may have a bluish cast due to sky reflection, and a correction filter will be needed. Another possibility – but a difficult one to control visually – is to use fill-in flash or strobe with the reflector pointed down at the shadow area (see later section on Flash and strobe, p. 32). The artificial light is then a secondary source, but it can also be a primary source if the entire area to be photographed is without ample natural light. For small shadowed sections, reflecting the sun's rays with crumpled aluminum foil over a piece of cardboard to support it makes a good reflecting surface, or a spread newspaper can do a surprisingly adequate job.

Textural effects are either accentuated or diminished by the type of illumination falling on the surfaces, and are seen most readily by strong contrasts of the raised lighter portions adjacent to the depressed shadow areas (see Plate 4). To show the texture most effectually, the afore-mentioned difference requires emphasis by creating bright highlights and heavy shadows, this being accomplished best by crosslighting (side-lighting). Shadowless light, as on a sunless day, would therefore not reveal texture very well, would give what is called a flat look to the surface, and such a picture usually lacks clarity of detail. Inscriptions are best revealed by sidelighting (see Plate 8).

Experience is the only real teacher with light, and the photographer needs to watch and record the varying light situations and see for himself what appears best, what light most effectively furnishes the desired outcomes; and then try with the camera to see if it happens. Herein lies the importance of the temporary notebook, for on a large excavation there are too many areas to trust to memory, and failure to note the prime time and have it slip by unproductively is a distinct loss, perhaps an irretrievable one. Of course the photographer may not always be able to wait for ideal conditions, so has to make do with the best available under less favorable circumstances. There are after all just so many digging days during a season, and time waits for no man – not even an archaeological photographer!

For color photography early morning light is (as was previously noted) most apt to be bluish, but late afternoon light is nearly always reddish, and attempting to balance these differences with color filters is a tricky business that requires a color meter and a wide range of varying compensating filters if color is a principle feature, such as in a wall painting or mosaic. To make matters worse we cannot really depend fully upon

our own eyes to give us an accurate color reading, for the eye adapts itself to colors by becoming less sensitive to the prevailing blue or red. During the middle of the day then, say from 10 to 3, is the most advantageous time as far as color balance is concerned. Unfortunately it may not be best for accentuating texture, unless perhaps when the sun is directly overhead in the case of a wall, or if the surface to be photographed happens to run at right angles to the sun – more or less north and south.

Attempting to shoot into the sun presents a particular difficulty, as vertical surfaces facing the camera will be in shadow. With this we have the same situation as discussed a bit back – diffused light, fill-in flash or strobe, or a reflector being the key. In addition the lens will have to be shielded carefully to prevent a flare that will fog the film.

EXPOSURE

Coupled with illumination is exposure control by the photographer. A well-known golden rule for the majority of photographing is 'expose for the shadow detail and let the highlights take care of themselves'. Notwithstanding its quite universal acceptance this principle often worries beginner photographers, as they feel that highlights can be important too – as indeed they can. But if one has to choose, one had better choose to get shadow detail. Actually most of today's black and white films have such wide latitudes that this problem is not as important as it once was. With color films, which have considerably less latitude, the rule has to be applied judiciously and supplemental light may be needed more frequently. In black and white the real secret of achieving a good spread of tones in a picture is also in the development of the negative and later in the printing (see Chapter 5, The Darkroom, p. 100), and it is well to know that a lack of contrast in areas can be partially corrected in processing. Long exposures may tend to halate or fog some films; therefore the shortest exposure that can do the job is always recommended.

Because in the Western world we read from left to right, the usual convention is to have light enter from the upper left part of the picture if possible – though obviously it is often impossible – but when there is any choice in the matter the upper left direction does seem a more natural one.

In warm climates the over-all brightness range is much greater than that upon which film manufacturers base average exposures, so it is

advisable to automatically decrease exposures by one-half to one full stop if going only by recommended setting and not by a meter, especially where there is brightly colored sand. The older selenium cell meters regularly read a bit low in bright light, and films do get a little more sensitive (hence faster) at higher temperatures, so even with a meter reading a decrease may be in order.

FLASH AND STROBE

Two unhappy designations used today are: *electronic flash* and *flash*. Actually both basic systems of auxiliary light are powered by electricity and both emit a flash of light. The word *strobe* clearly indicates its basic character, and so *flash* is applied quite inappropriately to the other system.

The need for flash or strobe will be dependent upon several factors, namely how much of an accessory light will be used, where, and for what reasons. Flash (using bulbs that fire but once) is certainly cheaper if required for only a limited number of occasions; it might even be less expensive for rather many occasions, but one must consider the bulk of the bulbs that have to be shipped, possibly to the point of them being unprofitable. Flash guns using the BC principle are most dependable and work on higher voltages. When there will be much demand for artificial light, as in underground tombs or cave interiors where there is apt to be no daylight at all, certainly the strobe is invaluable, may be with one or more supplemental slave units if the situation warrants. Strobe of course can be recharged where nickel cadmium batteries are the basic power (or even wet batteries), and the number of flashes is astronomically high. On the other hand power pack batteries usually need replacing after a given number of flashes, though some few units also can be recharged on an AC line. For overseas work one must be certain that any strobe or recharger unit has a built-in adjustment for handling different voltages which may be found in foreign countries. When fear about running out of bulbs is put aside, like films, there can be a great relief, and strobe units offer this assurance.

Probably the greatest use for strobe or flash will be as fill-in light to better illuminate areas or objects in shadow, such as in a pit or trench. Therefore a large and extremely powerful unit is uneconomical and heavy to carry around; rather a pocket-sized strobe is to be preferred, like the Heliotron/CC Supra that weighs only 14 oz and yet has a

Kodachrome guide number of 40–50, depending upon the surrounding reflecting surfaces. New strobe units should be tested to determine their individual working guide number, as many of the smaller units on the market tend to be overrated. Furthermore, the manufacturers set the guide numbers for average pictures, and earth as a reflecting surface is not average, for it soaks up much light. Adequate lengths of extension cords should be part of the equipment when several units are to be fired simultaneously or when the flash is to be used off camera. There are available, however, slave units which fire automatically by means of an electric eye when the main strobe is set off, and these need no extension wires.

With both flash and strobe it is difficult to predict how highlight and shadows will result in relation to the subject or area surrounding. Experience naturally does help one to know about highlights and shadows but never completely. This is why many commercial establishments use what is called modeling lights on the larger studio strobe units (or they stick to floods), but these are for indoor photography and do not work well outdoors, as the modeling lights are too weak in daylight to show the effect wanted. In dark areas of almost no natural light, either the flash gun or strobe unit can be fired a number of times successively (while the camera is on time or bulb) to illuminate large surfaces not covered adequately by a single burst of light. With flash the bulbs have to be changed and with strobe the unit has to recycle, so in either case some slight delay is necessary between firings. Strobe units recycle in anywhere from 3 to 15 seconds, depending upon the particular unit.

The color balance of flash and strobe are considerably different, clear flash bulbs being rated at 3,800°K, blue flash bulbs at 6,000°K, and strobe at 7,000°K, the latter two approximating daylight. With black and white films the color temperature is insignificant, but with color films the proper balance must be maintained for natural color, and filtration is necessary according to the kind of films or flash used. Compensating filters needed to restore the correct balance also cut down on the light level. Guide numbers and scales for flash bulbs are printed on their cartons; for strobe a scale is usually imprinted on or attached to the unit.

To achieve the proper ratio of fill-in to sunlight, the normal meter reading is taken, getting aperture and shutter speed settings. Then the distance in feet of the lamp-to-subject is calculated by dividing the exposure guide number by the lens opening. For example, the subject exposure calls for f/.16 at $\frac{1}{100}$ second; the flash bulb (or strobe) and film

33

combination gives a guide number of 160 at $\frac{1}{100}$ second; divide the latter guide number by the aperture: $160 \div 16 = 10$. At 10 ft the lamp's light will equal the sunlight and eliminate the sun's shadow. If a slight shadow is desired, the lamp can be moved back or a single thickness of a white handkerchief can be draped over the reflector. Each thickness of a handkerchief reduces the light intensity by about one f/stop.

Four precautions require attention: 1. extra batteries or powerpacks need to be protected from both excessive heat or dampness; 2. contacts on or in cameras may corrode in the tropics, so need to be cleaned periodically; 3. although most of the recently designed strobe units are safe, a few send enough current through the shutter contacts to cause arcing, thereby damaging those contacts – another item to check before purchasing; and 4. the capacitors of strobes˜need to be kept formed by continual use or by reforming with electricity. If no electricity is present, they can be kept in ready condition by firing them several times at intervals of not more than a week apart.

FILMS

Dyes in all color films will eventually fade, so the practice is to take all pictures in black and white and supplement these if possible and desirable with color shots. Though the fading of color is considerably less rapid than formerly, it is still a problem – in either transparencies or prints. Of course black and white prints fade too, but only extremely slowly if properly processed.

Films of the leading manufacturers are entirely reliable today (within their inherent limitations), and the photographer can depend upon consistent results if the materials are not subjected to excessive cold, heat, or humidity, and if proper care is taken in handling and processing. In general black and white films are less critical exposure-wise and have greater latitude than do color films, but there are exceptions. To get the best detail it is highly desirable that the grain characteristics be as small as possible (for both black and white and color films), so one would for the majority of purposes choose a slower rather than a higher speed film; yet the faster films have greater latitude. Hence the need for a compromise between slow and fast material for most of the work.

Films on the market will be selected largely as a result of experience to get the job done with the particular equipment on hand and considering the conditions under which they will be employed. This selection is

Plate 5. Archaeologist and helper taking measurements while themselves providing a scale

Plate 6.　Workmen repairing theater steps

Plate 7.   Use of sunlight for sculptural detail

Plate 8.   Sidelighting for lettering and texture detail

usually by the photographer himself, but other advice may well be sought. Some films come only in a limited number of sizes – not available for all cameras. Usually the view or press cameras of the 4 × 5-in. size allow the widest choices, these cameras being used more for commercial and professional tasks. However, one may not either want or require a whole raft of different films!

It is important to standardize by selecting a few types of films that can be expected to cover the foreseeable situations. Obviously the fewer the films that have to be taken along the simpler the task. Many films are still made specifically for certain effects, some recording continuous tones better than others, some showing up line work more clearly (as in maps and plans), and some being more sensitive to one color than another. In giving characteristics of outdoor films, manufacturers refer to average outdoor conditions, but the situations in which an archaeological photographer is likely to find himself are often far from average. Contrasting lighting in trenches, for instance, may call for less contrasty films and certainly less contrasty developers and printing papers, and this must be a consideration when ordering materials.

It also must be remembered that most expeditions are physically far removed from sources of film supply. Running short of films could be just as disastrous as a breakdown in camera equipment. Actually films are among the least expensive of the major items used, so stinting is a penny wise and pound foolish procedure. Better to return with unused films that undoubtedly will be needed for later work anyway than have to scrimp and develop ulcers rather than films while worrying about the diminishing stock. 'Will they stretch to the end?' is a question that should never need to be asked. Probably only by direct personal experience can one estimate how much of the various films to order and pack, and requirements will vary from place to place, even from year to year in the same location. If the photographer is new to the job, he will need to seek the advice of others familiar with the situation. Then there is the ever-present hazard of spoilage when the dig is situated in an area of perverse climatic conditions, and this calls for a reserve supply.

A familiar outcry can invariably be heard from any kind of photographer: 'Just one more, please!' Seemingly the photographer is never satisfied, but with good cause oftentimes. 'As much as I have photographed my various projects, as many individual pictures as I have made at each site, I have never made enough. Something always turns up before the dig is finished to make me wish that I had not neglected some specific angle.'[13]

Previously when discussing the choice of cameras the term *films* was used throughout rather than *plates,* and for a very specific and important reason. In the earlier days of archaeological photography, plates were the standard negative materials, plates being glass to which the emulsion adhered. Easier to use today and much less risky in the field are emulsions on a celluloid or other similar flexible bases, which are commonly referred to as films. Plates are emphatically not recommended today for field work, for glass breaks too easily, is heavier, and requires more bulky packing. Plates are still used commercially because of the flatness of their glass surfaces and their somewhat finer resolution, but both of these factors are more theoretical than practical with today's equipment in the field. The resolution of panchromatic sheet or roll films today is more than adequate for what is demanded by the photo-engraver and printing press. And no significant buckling arises in 4 × 5-in. or smaller sizes of films. Of course if one insists upon a larger size, this is a point of consideration; yet it is doubtful that even the 5 × 7-in. size would be so adversely affected as to require the disadvantages of using glass in the field.

Films, particularly color films, are subject to rapid deterioration, under inordinate amounts of humidity and heat, so those to be used in tropical areas must be purchased and retained in water-vapor-tight packages if they are to be kept in 70 per cent or higher humidity for longer than one week. Most Kodak films are packaged in such containers normally, though other manufacturers may or may not so pack their films – make sure! When 35-mm films are to be used the purchase of 20-exposure rolls is suggested rather than the 36, so that the films do not remain too long in the cameras. The recommendations published by Kodak in a free pamphlet, *Notes on Tropical Photography* (Publication No. C-24) available at Kodak Distribution Centers, must be read and strictly abided by. If a refrigerator is available, all sealed and unused films, except those to be put in the cameras immediately, should be stored in it – the cool chamber not the freezer! Films are then removed several hours in advance of use to gradually warm up, otherwise water will condense on their cool surfaces inside the camera. When feasible the films should be ordered in amounts permitting them to be shipped in their original factory-sealed packages as additional insurance against climatic conditions and accidents.

Incidentally if films are sent by mail outside of the country to be processed, always make certain to mark clearly on the outside of the package 'EXPOSED FILMS', else some conscientious customs inspector is

likely to slip it under an X-ray machine to check its contents and that will be the end of the films, or rather the images on them.

BLACK AND WHITE FILMS

Not all of the popular types of films are available for all types of cameras, but filters can often be used to alter their usual characteristics to achieve almost the same results as another kind or make. However, no filter should ever be employed without a definite purpose and where not necessary, so some judgment has to be made as to how many kinds of films are practical to carry, and if filters will serve rather than additional types of films. The choice may be an easy one with the miniature camera, since the variety of black and white films manufactured for the small camera is less than that for 4×5-in. sizes (but more than for roll film cameras); filters (and different developers) may have to substitute, especially for studio copying.

No attempt has been made to name specific brands of films, because of 1. the great number of emulsions that are similar but go under different trade names, and their use is largely by preference; and 2. the constantly changing characteristics of film manufactured – ASA speeds and other factors being altered frequently. There are many fine films manufactured by a number of film makers, and there are nearly always emulsions available with equivalent or similar characteristic made by several firms.

In general the basic black and white film material recommended for most archaeological work is a medium speed panchromatic film, though smaller amounts of others could be considered for special purpose work.

COLOR FILMS

Unless the fading problem is substantially licked, it is probable that color films will never fully replace black and white in the foreseeable future, particularly for record purposes. With Polaroid Color (Polacolor) it is however now possible to actually do all outdoor photography for prints in color, and the increasing use of color transparencies and prints by the general public has contributed much to hasten this development of color. Even today it is likely that an expedition will need some, perhaps a good deal of color photography for publication, exhibition, and lecture purposes. This undoubtedly means at least one more camera, though certainly color films are available in sheets and so can be loaded in sheet film holders reserved for that special need. But sheet films in color (even

Polacolor) are still beyond the budgets of many archaeological teams – except possibly in very limited quantities. A smaller camera is the answer therefore to do the color work simply as an economy measure (but don't ignore the cost of an additional camera if one is not already available). There may already be a miniature or roll film camera in use or contemplated for black and white, so another body of the same model would be a good choice – unless the camera is a Contarex, Contaflex, Hasselblad, or Bronica, all of which have interchangeable backs for different films.

Color films (exclusive of Polacolor) present several difficult problems in the field not applicable to black and white films, not the least important of which is processing. It is rarely possible to have conditions exacting enough on location to process color films right, for the demands of the films are too stringent, notably in regard to temperature control of the solutions that must be kept within a half degree, plus or minus, of the manufacturer's stated figure. And not being able to process the film results in a second problem: how to keep exposed films from deteriorating? Conditions of heat and humidity in overpowering amounts are bad enough to try and keep sealed and unused films from spoiling, but upon exposed films these conditions can be ruinous. In many places to trust films to the handling of the local post, assuming it can be mailed to some not too distant lab, might be just as disastrous, for mail boxes or carrier pouches often sit for hours in the hot sun. Unless mailing under good conditions is certain, the exposed films should be resealed and stored in a refrigerator or ice chest after being treated with a desiccating agent. Without this latter treatment one is courting danger, however, for humidity would undoubtedly have worked into the film during its use, and resealing the films with moisture inside, even at low temperatures, is certainly, to put it mildly, not the preferred practice!

For the same reasons as with the preceding section about black and white films, no specific brands of color films are named here, but it should be noted that there are two basic types generally available: reversal and negative-positive. The first produces a so-called transparency for projection purposes, while the second produces a color negative from which positive color prints may be made.

POLAROID FILMS

Though presently more costly than comparable amounts of standard black and white films (including processing charges), the advantages of

almost immediately seeing the results in print form and the uncomplicatedness of the method offer a tremendous advantage to these materials. With color, size for size, and taking into account processing and printing of the usual color materials, there is even less of a price differential than with black and white, although it must be remembered that as yet only Polacolor prints are possible – no negatives. Undoubtedly the near future will bring a color negative type as it did black and white, and thus make the Polaroid process even more valuable.

Probably the better system of using Polaroid materials is in an adapter for a 4 × 5-in. camera rather than in one of the series of Polaroid Land cameras, the latter having no distortion controls and a not completely satisfactory viewing system for archaeological work. The Polaroid Land 4 × 5-in. Holder fits any camera of that size with the Graflok-type back. The size 4 × 5 in. is somewhat misleading, as the actual dimensions turn out to be $3\frac{1}{2}$ × $4\frac{1}{2}$ in., not all of the area being used for the picture (a white border surrounds the picture area on the print).

Contrast control is possible with Polaroid's black and white 4 × 5-in. films (except Type 55 P/N) simply by varying the development time; the shorter the development period the less contrasty will be the print. Exposure latitude and resolution is good, and there is virtually no visible grain.

Just as with standard films the kind of work to be done will accordingly dictate the film type. When a number of substantial enlargements are contemplated the 55 P/N (black and white) will be the choice, because it yields both a fast positive proof and a negative. All that is needed by way of processing the negative is to clear, wash, and dry it, the first step using an 18 per cent sodium sulfite solution.

While development time is not critical with Polacolor, the ASA speed rating varies considerably with the temperature, high when the weather is hot and low when it is cold. So far the film is available only in the Daylight-type emulsion, and shutter speeds at less than $\frac{1}{10}$ second result in both a loss of speed and a shift toward the yellow. Therefore the usual indoor light situations (except strobe or blue flash) is questionable. Unlike the black and white Polaroid materials, Polacolor is not hand coated with a fixative after development.

Black and white transparencies are possible with a special Polaroid film (as noted earlier); however, if 2 × 2-in. slides are wanted, the 4 × 5-in. film has to be used, and since the entire area of the film is not utilized, this results in a telephoto effect. The transparency material fits Polaroid Roll Film Backs, special adapters like the Land 4 × 5-in.

Holders that slide into the rear of standard 4 × 5-in. view or press cameras.

OTHER SPECIALIZED FILMS
Movie films, infrared films, ultraviolet films, and X-ray films are included in Chapter 4 where their use is detailed.

FILTERS

Mentioned previously but worth repeating is the rule that no filter should be used without a purpose and where not necessary, the reason being that dust or possible scratches and smudges on filters do affect the image, however slight; and reflections off their surfaces, even if coated, can cause minute amounts of fogging to the film. In most instances such effects will go unnoticed, but the reason for the rule is still a sound one.

Figure 4. Types of filters for photographic use
Note: some are used for black and white only, some for color only, some for both, and there is an overlapping of uses.

Filter type	Use
correction or compensating	to produce tones as seen by the eye
contrast	to distort tones for emphasis
haze	to reduce aerial haze
neutral density	to increase exposure time
polarizing	to polarize sunlight or lamps

There are five general types of filters for black and white and color photography (see fig. 4). Cheap though they are, filters are nevertheless important and must be selected with care – and then only after the camera's lenses have been chosen, so that the right diameter is obtained. Different focal length lenses usually will have different front diameters, and therefore take different series size filters. The need for duplicating filters in various sizes for the different lenses often can be avoided by the employment of a series of step-up rings which screw into the filter holder, the latter purchased to fit the various diameters. Filters can then be secured to fit the largest diameter lens. Most modern lenses are internally threaded at their opening, and filter holders are manufactured

in many sizes to fit practically any known lens diameter. Combinations of retaining rings are also needed in the event that two filters are required at one time, say a color filter and a plus lens. On the front filter holder is screwed or clamped a sunshade, and care must be exercised to choose the shade which will not vignette the shortest focal length lens, especially if in front of several filter holders, though the latter may just as effectively serve as a sunshade. However, a sunshade is needed to shield the filters as well as the lens. When threaded filter holders are either not found or not wanted, a type with adjustable flanges that hold by friction can be purchased.

In times past some photographers put their filters on the rear of their lenses (inside the camera) rather than on the front, the reason being that the lens cap was employed for controlling the exposure instead of the shutter, and filters just got in the way if in front; but, with today's faster films and lenses, this seems a needless and unnecessarily time-consuming procedure (even if possible), since attempting to focus with a dark filter on, for instance, presents a singular hardship when the filter is attached inside the camera. Naturally this older system is not workable with other than view cameras.

Gelatin filters are available, but optical glass ones seem to be more durable in the field despite the fact that they are of glass. By all means purchase filters in metal rims when available, the metal affording some measure of protection if filters are dropped on their edges.

Figure 5.   Filters, factors, and effects upon skies with pan films
Note: K2, G, and A filters also reduce atmospheric haze in that order, A being the most effective.

Filter	Factor	Sky effect
none		lighter than normal
K2 (yellow)	2 ×	normal
G (orange)	3 ×	darker than normal
A (red)	8 ×	dramatically dark

General views are enhanced by proper lighting and often by proper filtration. For black and white photography the K2 (yellow) or A (red) filters darken the sky value while leaving the clouds (if any) light (see fig. 5). The contrast between a dark sky and light clouds heightens the visual appeal of panoramic pictures and those which may include architectural details in the foreground. For color photographs the

polarizing filter will do the same if shot at about a 90° angle away from the sun. An advantage of the polarizing filter is that by rotating its axis, various degrees of darkening are possible. At full polarization the filter factor is 3 to 4, somewhat less when rotated to a lesser degree of polarization. Often a haze will partially obscure the definition of distant objects, the aforementioned filter helping to penetrate it and making details more distinct.

Filters may be needed to alter colors of objects, stratifications, etc. (see fig. 6). In addition to these already mentioned, neutral density filters #1 or #2 can be used to increase exposure time when high speed films require it.

Figure 6. Filters, factors, and effects upon colors with pan films
Note: to make colors seem normal a K2 filter may be needed (2 × factor).

Filter	Factor	Lighter	Darker
A (red)	8 ×	red	blue and green
B (green)	8 ×	green	blue and red
C5 (blue)	5 ×	blue	red and green
G (orange)	3 ×	red and green	blue

Films that may be needed for correcting color balance in color photography are: 1. 80B, 80C, 82C, and 82A (blue filters, dark to light respectively); 2. 81A, 81C, 85C, 85, 85B (red filters, light to dark respectively); 3. polarizing filter; and 4. haze or UV filter (to cut through atmospheric haze or protect the lens from dust or salt water). The blue filters given above can also be used to correct excessive reddishness in late afternoon, while the red filters can correct too much blueness on cloudy days, in the shade, or in the early morning (in dry and waste areas dust may make sunlight slightly red in the morning hours rather than blue). To find which compensating filter is necessary for a specific film under a specific type of lighting, reference to the Light Balancing Dial found in Kodak's *Master Photoguide* (Publication No. R-21) is suggested.

Polaroid or Polacolor films use the same filters as do standard materials, since the black and white films are a pan type and the color film is similar in characteristics to other daylight color films.

Cases for filters, like those discussed in the section about plus lenses, can be improvised if no combination holders are readily available, or if it is desirable to make a more compact case. Instruction sheets packaged

with the original filters can be preserved and used as references for functions and recommended increases in exposure times.

FIELD SCALES

Nearly all archaeologists suggest that every picture taken in the field for archaeological purposes should contain a scale of some kind – not necessarily a scale stick or rod, but a human figure or a familiar object such as a trowel can do very well at times and may even be preferable for many purposes. In a burial pit or mound an adult human skeleton fulfills the same function. Publicity pictures should invariably contain a figure or part of one as a means of human interest – the connecting of the past to the present. Scale sticks for publicity pictures probably should be eliminated, since despite attempts at making them seem inconspicuous, they never quite make it and do detract from the artistic aspects so desirable in such shots. On the other hand a picture with a scale stick in it seems to have a certain appeal to the layman as being the 'real thing', and may therefore not be so objectionable as might be imagined. In the last analysis there is probably no hard and fast rule in publicity pictures. But there is one rule that must be adhered to for these pictures and that is when people are used as scales they should appear as in candid pictures – not standing like bumps on a log and gawking at the camera, but doing something that ties them relatively to the subject, their faces always directed at the subject (see plates 5 and 6).

A scientific record, which archaeology attempts, demands correct use of an accurate scale, this being as true for general views as for close-ups, for wide-angle shots as for telephoto ones. While trees, buildings, and other objects may give a rough idea of scale, they are not nearly exact enough. It was for this reason that scale sticks were devised, marked off in identical sections of known dimension. The actual length of the stick or rod used will vary with the area or object to be included in the picture – long sticks for general views, shorter ones for close-ups. In fact three or four variations in length are frequently used at a site, three probably being the minimum. A long rod of 6–8 ft serves to scale whole trenches and sizable excavations; a medium size of 2 or 3 ft would be suitable for an area of around 6 ft in diameter; while a one-foot rule would suffice for small objects, though a four to six-inch rule will often come in handy. Of course these might be divided into meters or centimeters rather than feet or inches, and the photographer would have to know the standard

customarily employed at the location before preparing his own. And the photographer should have his own scales, guarding them jealously to keep them from getting scarred through indiscriminate handling by other people. It is even a wise precaution to keep the scales encased in some protective sheath-like covering when not in use.

The larger rods are usually made of 1×1 in. seasoned lumber, square or octagonal, though aluminum poles are now finding use at many places because of their lightness and durability. An easy method of painting the divisions is first to coat the entire length with white paint, mask off alternating divisions with tape, and then paint or spray the pole black (or red). When the masking tape is removed, the result will be alternating stripes of white and black (or red). The bottom unit can be further subdivided in equal parts: tenths in the case of meters or twelfths in the case of feet.

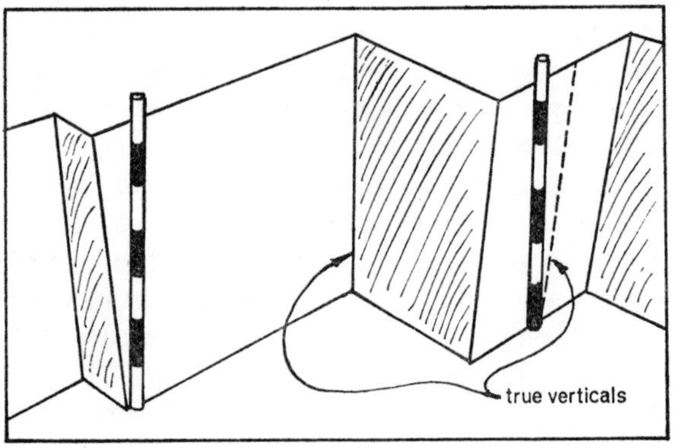

Figure 7. High-angle view
Note: if the scale stick is lined up along the true vertical, the top edge of the trench would be somewhat lower on the stick's marking. The only position where it would not read falsely is the corner of the trench in the exact center.

As noted earlier the stick should be placed in as unobtrusive position as possible, certainly not monopolizing the attention or unnecessarily directing it away from what is the real subject. However, in large views as many as three sticks (or figures) may be deemed essential to provide the proper scale to the various dimensions at different distances from the camera. For small subjects care must be observed in placing the rule on the same plane as the center of the object (or as close to it as is feasible), else a false sense of scale can be conveyed.

Archaeologists have invariably demanded that upright scale sticks in

pictures be precisely vertical – parallel according to the sides of the print. The reason for this has to be aesthetic, for a moment's reflection will result in the admission that a vertical rule can be inaccurate when walls are perspectively slanted as in the accompanying diagram (see fig. 7). In the face of a cry for accuracy in the field, it is a bit difficult to defend this inconsistency, even though the discrepancy is usually not of very great proportions. Yet the practice persists, though it is not often faced up to. There are two solutions: 1. use the camera in such a way that only true verticals will result (though the necessary manipulation in the correction of linear distortion may introduce other falsifications); or 2. let the stick tilt as it may but let everybody know by practice that it is vertical with the wall or whatever. Undoubtedly it will be quite some time before either development becomes universal.

For convenience, conversion tables in changing from U.S. to metric measurements are found in Appendix B.

THE FIELD NOTEBOOK

No matter how dependably excellent are the photographs, without proper records they may be almost useless. Archaeological photographers maintain that every frame of film exposed, whether in the field, studio, or some other location, should be recorded. In general this is true except that, if one is using a miniature camera, a single notation might do for a number of frames taken in close sequence of the same subject – unless there is a decided change in direction, exposure, or some other significant factor.

Pictures taken in the field are recorded in the photographer's field notebook and correlated with the site recorder's journal and/or register. The recorder is trained to note in his book what pictures are taken of a particular subject. Not only does this system provide for a cross-checking by the team of items photographed, but it also serves as a reference by the photographer for lighting and exposure data in later pictures where the conditions are similar.

Physically the notebook should be a hard-cover, bound book rather than a looseleaf variety, for the pages tend to tear free no matter how well reinforced, and in the middle of a shrieking gale this can be devilishly annoying. If the photographer feels that this system is not conducive to neatness, the material can be copied into another book in his spare time (of which there isn't any!). Incidentally the ballpoint pen has

become a fast friend of the archaeologist, principally because of its non-leaking ink supply and almost indestructible point. Several pens and refills should be a part of the photographer's personal gear. The book size would be an individual choice, conditional upon whether it is to be kept in the pocket, in a pouch on the belt, or in the camera gadget bag. I favor the pouch idea. For a small pocket or pouch-sized book, a rubber stamp made for imprinting a chart to be filled in with a pen is a possibility, or pages can be mimeographed with a chart thereon and bound together in book form. The latter allows for a somewhat larger chart (see fig. 8).

19 67 site/sec/level	time/light	exposure	registry
OPAL/A/II/6 LOOKING SW CORNER W/POT#2621 7/12/67	2:45pm CLOUDY SUBJ. IN SHADE STROBE #1 AT 3'	CAMERA B 150mm LENS K2 FILTER f/32 -1/60sec PAN-X	N.B.108, p.63 DRWG #316 NEG #F1053 UNDER EXP.– SEE #F1062

Figure 8.   Page of photographer's field notebook
Note: the *site/sec/level* column should also include the approximate taking directions, any important identifying objects and date; the *time/light* refers to the time of day and lighting, natural or artificial; *exposure* includes camera, lens, filters, diaphram opening, shutter speed (or time exposure), and film; *registry* is keyed to the site recorder's book with page and drawing numbers and another number which is the sequence number of the negative (F denotes 'field' to distinguish it from some other picture location), and there should also be an indication as to the negative's useability. Abbreviations can be used to conserve space, but they should be consistent and noted in the front of the notebook in the event that other persons need to interpret them.

As referred to earlier there should be in addition a temporary notebook for rough notes about lighting and other conditions in specific locations. A small spiral-bound notebook will satisfy this requirement.

SIGNBOARDS OR MARKERS

Site directors may also insist on a signboard being placed near objects or areas photographed as a double check or in the eventuality that written records become lost. Especially with small-negative photo-

graphy, where information cannot easily be penned on the margin of the negative, this system is helpful. Such signboards are simple to procure or make. Available in sets are white plastic letters that can be affixed in the horizontal grooves of a black felt-covered board. Still another system uses sets of plaster letters with pins imbedded in their backs that can be stuck into a backing surface of some kind. But a slate and chalk may be the most satisfactory, since the letters of sets just mentioned tend to get lost, soiled, or broken easily in the field. The possible messy appearance of the chalkboard is of no more consequence here than it is in Hollywood, as the board in archaeological pictures is placed well at the side so that it can be cropped out from prints for publication. On the signboard goes such items as site, trench, level, date, or any other clarifying information. The main point to observe is that letters or numbers placed on the board are made sufficiently large to show up properly in a 4 × 5-in. print.

Where there is no signboard, then an identification card is often propped up so that it can be seen plainly in the printed photograph. Lacking such a card the site notebook can be spread open and lettered across its pages.

FIELD KIT

In a small metal box the following list of tools and supplies necessary for work in the field should be assembled:

Plasticine (*for propping up objects or holding them together temporarily*)
plumb bob and line (*for getting centered vertically over an object*)
small scissors
penknife
flat-bladed knife
tablespoon
1-in. and 2-in. paint brushes
#6 camel's hair brush
small whisk broom
small trowel
small scale sticks
metal tape measure (*circular – in inches and centimeters*)
white chalk
small dustpan (*child's toy size*)
possibly a signboard with letters or chalkboard

CLEANLINESS OF SITE

A good archaeological photograph of the dig is contingent upon many factors some of which may seem trivial to the uninitiated. Experienced photographers, though, have discovered that cleanliness of the site is not really so trivial, for only by this means can photographic separation of horizontals and verticals, clear texture, and distinct edges or corners be defined. Workmen have to be patiently trained to do this, mostly interested as they are in merely digging and uncovering. Careful brushing away of sand or dirt, the pruning of overhanging grass (if any), the washing of outcropping stones, etc., is likely to represent for them just time lost and quite a dull procedure. Site directors, however, have come to understand the value of such cleanliness and order, particularly since extensive commercial publishing of pictures has become the rule rather than the exception. A well-cleaned site allows for better definition of contours of objects, rocks, or whatever with the camera, and shows up tonal differences more satisfactorily (again refer to Plates 1 and 2). Unfortunately some directors have little foresight by permitting dumpings to confuse the area that will eventually need to be photographed, and part of the photographer's job may be to suggest tactfully a better place for them. Tools, temporarily discarded clothing, a jeep, the site desk, a surveying table, or other miscellaneous items extraneous to the photo have to be removed before the picture is taken, otherwise these things not only will be an unsightly clutter, but, more important, they will detract from the intended subject. Finds *in situ* require preliminary cleansing, even though they are fragile, for a photographic record of such finds may be the only one obtained if something unforseen occurs to destroy the objects during their removal.

Whether or not the site director will trust the photographer to do the job of cleaning of objects or preparing stratifications for good recording, depends largely upon his confidence in the photographer. If he has found by experience that the photographer is capable of doing these things, then only a simple agreement on procedure is necessary, but the photographer must always first get clearance. This is a firm must.

SPECIAL SITUATIONS AND FINDS

So far the writing has referred to quite general conditions at a site, but inevitably some specialized situations will arise demanding specific

approaches. At the same time undoubtedly a number of artifacts will be uncovered whose substances may vary considerably and which may also require rather individual attention. 'Special features to be emphasized in the photograph', notes Atkinson, 'should be marked with arrows or circles cut out of a white card.'[14] Such a procedure is frequently a good plan for at least one picture, but even more than scale sticks such markers do tend to detract from the aesthetic appearance.

The standard work for treatment and care of various materials (metals, clays, etc.) found in archaeological locations is a 1962 edition of H. J. Plenderleith's book *The Conservation of Antiques and Works of Art; Treatment, Repair, and Restoration* (Oxford University Press).

UNDERGROUND TOMBS AND CAVE INTERIORS

In neither of these two places can the photographer count upon sufficient daylight for adequate pictures. Unless large areas of the tomb's roof have been removed, or if the cave is very shallow, artificial light will be needed (see Plate 9). And most likely multiple flash or strobe will be the only sensible answer (the days of magnesium strips and flash powder for illumination are gone!). Cave walls will ordinarily be quite rough and thus absorb a large amount of light; while tomb walls are more usually smooth, even polished, possibly with paintings or bas-relief sculpture. Exterior pictures of both places will also be wanted for the record even if of no architectural significance. And for caves which may be rather high up from the ground level a telephoto lens is utterly indispensable for picturing the outside.

SOIL STRATIFICATION

In cutting trenches the general practice for shallow cuts of up to about eight feet in depth is to dig perpendicular sides, but in the interests of safety deeper cuts are made with sides on a batter (slight angle). With sides on a batter the pitch of their surfaces reflects more light and makes for easier photographing as far as illumination is concerned, but this does compound the distortion of angles in terms of linear perspective when true verticals are sought. Damp soils cut cleanly; dry soils present problems of crumbling that produce something less than sharp edges and clean surfaces.

Thousands of varieties of soils exist around the world: humus, loam, sand, clay, chalk, soil with rocks, without rocks, with minerals, etc. Though some resemble others closely and require microscopic examination to differentiate among them, each has specific and identifiable characteristics. However, in archaeological work it is often the case that layer upon layer of similar soils are consecutively laid down in an area, making it next to impossible to see any line of demarcation – to say nothing about attempting to photograph them. And there frequently is a perplexing lack of distinction between a stratum of man-made deposits and the natural stratum beneath.

A prime objective of archaeology is to distinguish among strata as a means of identifying and dating layers, and it is the photographer's job to record the layers visually each differentiated from the other. This is frequently quite a task, for strata easily seen as separate by the human eye may merge on the camera's black and white film. Color films of course record them like the eye sees them, and in this respect the color films are invaluable tools.

After the cutting has taken place, it is usually necessary to 'prepare' the section's surface for the photographs – to make the stratification more discernible in the picture. At the risk of overemphasis here is a pertinent quotation: 'A photograph of an uncleaned subject is a photograph wasted'.[15] Another author says, 'no amount of mechanical skill is a substitute for the careful preparation of the subject . . . a spotlessly clean trench is no mere "eye-wash", if only because it gives the spectator a justifiable trust in the orderliness and accuracy of the work'.[16] While the cleaning job may be done sometimes by workmen, it often falls to the lot of the photographer, for he knows exactly what he wants; and it is as true here as it is of many other things, 'if you want it done right, do it yourself!' Again let me caution that such preparation must be done only with the approval of the site director.

Preparation always begins at the top and works downward, so falling soil or cleanings will not obviate work already completed. First the angle at the top should be sharp. Then the first layer is scraped and brushed flat with a stiff brush. Stone or other imbedded materials are carefully cut around, so that these foreign stuffs project slightly and will cast shadows to aid in texture and identification. In fact stone surfaces of any size ought to be washed clean. If the soil has dried out but normally is damp, the mere scraping off of a thin layer with the trowel will 'freshen' it up; but, if the soil is naturally dry, water may have to be sprayed on the surface with a garden plant-spraying device to prevent it crumbling

and drifting to the bottom. Stratum by stratum downward the surface is readied until the floor is reached, whereupon the accumulated debris is shoveled away. Naturally before the soil dries out again the pictures should be taken.

When layers are substantially the same in texture and color, there are several ways to create visual differences: 1. slightly undercutting the upper stratum, thus causing a shadow to form (see fig. 9); 2. brushing

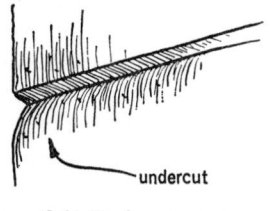

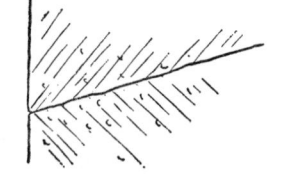

Figure 9. (*left*) Undercut stratum

Figure 10. (*right*) Brushed strata
Note: this works best with clay.

the soil of one stratum in a diagonal left to right and the other layer in the opposite direction (see fig. 10); 3. slightly polishing the surface of one layer by a rotary rubbing motion (particularly feasible with moist soil or clay); 4. dampening alternate layers with a spray of water; 5. making a line with the tip of the trowel between the strata; or 6. using a white tape if the strata are straight. Atkinson recommends[17] that the edges of pits and other depressions which are not very distinct should be marked with a narrow band of dark earth. '. . . The preparation of a subject occupies hours, occasionally days, before the brief session with the camera. Innumerable slipshod and uninformative photographs in excavation reports prove that this elaborate preparation is not unnecessary.'[18]

Recording the coloration of soils can be a difficult problem for black and white photography, but filtration can sometimes assist in distinguishing among layers if the strata are composed of different substances but appear quite alike to the eye. With panchromatic films an A (red) filter creates different tonal values between reddish and blackish soils that might otherwise look similarly gray in the picture. This filter lightens both red and yellow while it darkens green and blue. Looking through such a filter may give some idea of what happens to the film but not completely so. With color films no colored filter can be used that will not change the complete color balance except neutral density and

polarizing filters – the latter are additionally valuable in cutting sheen on a surface, either of soil or of an artifact.

WALLS

The preparation of uncovered man-made walls is also a matter of careful cleaning, though the surfaces are not usually scraped away as with soil. Rather the mud (if any) after drying is brushed away from the wall surface, whether the latter is composed of logs, sod, brick, stone, cement, stucco, tile, or some other material; and the courses between the basic substance are treated similarly. Some wall courses are of mortar; some have no mortar whatsoever. To produce acceptable detail in the photo meticulous attention must be given to this cleaning, a careless job of preparation being completely obvious to any person skilled in reading an archaeological photograph and perhaps even obvious to anyone else. In sun-dried brick walls the courses are often indistinct and one may have to resort to some undercutting of the mud brick. Sod walls are normally erected without courses as such, but at any rate the sod will be found packed together so solidly that it is practically impossible to tell where one piece leaves off and another begins. Plaster walls are likely to be dull and perhaps discolored. When dry they are more easily cleaned, but to photograph them they may require dampening if not too friable.

ROADS

Uncovered roads paved with logs, stone, brick, or merely trampled down, require a comparable treatment to the foregoing method of caring for walls, although horizontal surfaces of roads can usually stand a good deal more vigorous scrubbing than vertical walls. Lighting is more difficult for the photographer, however, unless the road is near the surface where a low-angle sun on the individual pieces of material can cast shadows to aid in their definition. Even better than crosslighting for a rough road is backlighting, but sunlight must be prevented from entering into the camera lens directly.

POTTERY

Pieces of ancient pottery found in or about digs usually are quite indestructible and are among the most common finds in many areas. Often the potsherds are discovered in great profusion, such as at Wetherill Mesa, Colorado, where over 750,000 were gathered from 1958 to 1963.[19] Nevertheless, there are great variations in substance and hardness, depending upon the adhesive quality of the soil and type of hardening

process used. Sun-hardened clay naturally would be easily destroyed, but flame or oven-fired clays are extremely durable – this is particularly true of the latter. Most pottery can withstand a thorough washing and not have either its substances or surface quality harmed, unless of course the clay happens to be painted, and then the decision to wash or not may hinge upon whether the decoration is glazed or just overpainted on a porous or semi-porous surface that has not been glazed. Obviously the last-mentioned demands delicate treatment, perhaps no washing at all. When the sherds are uncovered a photo should be taken of them *in situ*, and it is valuable for the photographer to know how they were made. Each piece to be pictured should at least be brushed free of dirt and, if feasible, washed and then placed back in the exact spot. In this way not only the sherds themselves will be seen better because of their cleaner appearance, but removing them and replacing them does a service in partially separating them visually from their surrounding matrix. This will show their edges more clearly and a slight shadow will set them off three-dimensionally from the soil. Obviously this cannot be done for each and every one of perhaps thousands of sherds, though some few may be of special interest for one reason or another. Certainly a whole pot or even a cracked but intact one could be worth a picture, though, if the latter, it must be photographed before removal. In this case a little careful brushing and possibly washing in place is called for, though marks of water spatterings on the surrounding area must be brushed away. On an expedition of any size there will be a pottery expert who reasonably may want to do the cleaning, which is just as well for the photographer, as the weighty responsibility can be a bit nerve-racking. The expert if busy can at least advise on what should be done.

When the surface is found to be painted some filters may be required to differentiate among colors for black and white pictures; and the previous section on filters gives the details. Unless the daylight is quite shadowless, reflectors are recommended for the dark side of the ceramic. Some amount of diffusion of light can be obtained by stretching cheese-cloth over the area in a kind of tent or tarp-like way. Shadow areas on the object may also be lightened in tone by running some white chalk over the finger and transferring this to the surface of the pottery. The angle of the photo will partly depend upon the angle of the piece itself relative to the horizontal. Several views of the subject may be desirable, particularly if its surface is decorated. Not all pottery is of ceramic material; some ancient ware may be in stone. Treatment and photography is similar, except that the grain or stratification in the stone (if any)

requires close attention. Ceramics found in burials may hold items like grain and pollen, which in themselves are important, though these will need to be photographed in the studio (see Chapter 4, under Photomicrography, p. 96).

For the picturing of single small objects like bowls or vases the temptation is to get up as close as possible with the camera in order to fill the frame; but this is usually an error, a longer focal length lens being the best to produce the truest profile. Another error is to photograph bowls or other round objects from an angle too high, since this also will distort the profiles – unless several pictures are made of the objects. Exposure for extreme close-ups of small objects where the lens is extended must be increased, and a method of computing this increase is found in Chapter 3, under Exposure, p. 77).

TEXTILES

Textiles are extremely perishable and when of any considerable age are likely to be found only in dry soils, in tombs without moisture, or where some peculiar condition has prohibited or retarded the decaying process. Since these textiles simply may fall apart in the attempt to lift them, 'photographed as found' is a must – with, however, some prudent brushing. And, because textiles are usually a rarity in excavations, the opportunity for photographs of them is seldom passed up. Filters may be indicated for correct color rendition of designs in black and white. Properly directed lighting plays an important part in their recording, perhaps more so than with most other materials *in situ*, for low-level crosslighting is necessary to bring out the texture, yet any decoration also should show clearly. A strobe or flash can be an invaluable asset at this point, as the sun cannot be counted on to furnish the necessary kind of illumination, the artificial light being portable and the sun not, though a mirror reflector can be used to channel the sun's rays at a low angle if the textile is not too large.

Rope, feathers, and feather mosaics present similar problems and requirements to textiles, all being highly friable and having strong texture detail that needs to be recorded.

BASKETWORK

Basketry offers analogous problems to pottery except that cane, grass, or reed are perishable in damp soils. If the basket weave is intact at all, the chances are that it can be cleaned quite readily with liquid castile soap. When decoration appears on it, either dye or different colored

materials have been employed, and accordingly the treatment may differ. Dye often fades upon exposure to light and so dyed designs are worn off if the basket material is close-grained and not particularly porous. Therefore caution is advised in handling and cleaning.

GLASS

Glass (actually a compound of metal) is most easily shattered into small bits, so it is seldom found completely whole except when it has been sealed in tombs where no soil or other material has crushed it. Glass is also highly difficult as a subject to photograph and obtain any semblance of faithfulness of reproduction, either in texture or color, since it varies in both. Knowledgeable lighting is the greatest help. Decomposed glass (such as old Roman glass often is) frequently has an iridescent surface, and the successful recording of this phenomenon requires considerable expertise. Different types of surfaces exist, i.e. frosted, reticulated, opaque, translucent, clear, and so on, each of which calls for somewhat modified changes in lighting, and only by experience can one learn what these changes are. A fair percentage of glass will be decorated by either glazing or sculpturing, relief or incising. Great caution must attend its cleaning, and there may be detail which can only be brought out in the photograph by cleaning the cracks and crevices with a knife. In some few instances water is detrimental to decomposed glass, so an expert ought either to do the cleaning or closely supervise it. In fact the iridescence of ancient Roman glass may flake off to the touch of a finger.

Glass can be found in the form of beads or other types of jewelry, but the same general procedure is indicated, except that the wire or other material upon which the glass might have been strung may have perished, and the position of each piece of glass as found is significant to later restoration. Glass or glass paste may be inset in jewelry, and the many chinks of the latter demand fastidious cleansing.

METALWORK

The method of cleaning metal will be dictated by the individual piece, and this job should be left to an expert. In the field such cleaning is confined usually to brushwork, but there are exceptions, gold being one. Corroded conditions of the metals tend to camouflage the shape or nature of objects, be they jewelry, weapons, or other forms of an intricate sort, so any cleaning at all, if not overdone, is welcome.

Items of iron or copper base can be partly cleaned by boiling them in

a 5–10 per cent solution of caustic soda and granulated zinc; silver base items in a 10 per cent solution of ammonia. Gold normally needs no treatment, as it neither corrodes nor tarnishes, though surface discolorations can be removed with the aforementioned ammonia solution. The use of just warm soapy water and a stiff brush is no longer recommended, according to Rhys Carpenter,[20] for in removing the surface crust, the destruction of the outermost layer occurs. The newest method is to immerse the object in an electrolytic bath of dilute caustic soda or other appropriate medium. 'The incrustation characteristic of ancient bronze is the result of oxidation. . . . Where this formation has been built up progressively without further damage to the surface structure, all of the original metal will still be present, though its outer layer will have been chemically converted from pure metal into that metal's oxide.'[21] The author then states[22] that this process of conversion can be reversed by reducing the oxide to pure metal, the corroded surface resuming its original smoothness.

If any of the foregoing is done and the item is returned for photographing to its location where found, it could look absurdly false, as nearly anyone knows that a freshly dug up metal object would never appear bright and clean (except gold). This problem of falsification is one with which the photographer must continually struggle at all times and with all pictures in the field.

WALL PAINTINGS

Throughout the history of art quite a variety of wall painting techniques have been developed, some made directly on a base material like stone, but most surviving to the present were painted on cement, stucco, or plaster, mainly the last. Some wall decorations have been painted on dry plaster (called *secco*), as they were in Egypt; others were made on fresh unset plaster (called *fresco*) like those on Crete; while also there have been numerous combinations and variations of these and other ingredients. It can be understood readily enough how secco wall paintings are more perishable, as the pigment flakes or wears off the surface; on the other hand fresco paintings are actually an integral part of the wall, since the pigment has permeated into the plaster. For cleaning purposes water may be injurious to dry wall paintings, but fresco paintings usually can stand washing, assuming not too much pressure is applied and it's not done too often. Sometimes the surface will have to be cleaned by light scraping if other less drastic methods fail.

When the wall paintings are considered of value, the wall itself may

be extricated from its location and there is the usual chance of it breaking up; so no moving is attempted before ample photos have been secured, both general and close-up details. General photos of the paintings should reveal the location of that painting relative to the whole wall and perhaps the entire building. Dampening with water also makes the colors seem fresher for photographic purposes, but since water dries rapidly – in hot climates particularly – a few drops of glycerin are added to delay the evaporation process. Again various filters can be used to increase contrast between colors for black and white photos. As an example a washed-out red can be strengthened with a B (green) filter (orthochromatic films will do a good job with reds in the same way but without needing a filter).

MOSAICS

Mosaics have been made on walls and ceilings, as well as on portable objects, but the majority found in excavations are pavements. Cleaning of the tesserae prior to photographing them presents the most time-consuming of efforts, for in the majority of instances dirt or mud must be removed with extreme caution, otherwise the little cubes are likely to be unseated as a result of age. Larger amounts of water may further loosen them so they almost have to be cleaned inch-by-inch, a tedious task. Detergents can be useful in removing original surface stains or soot.

If the mosaics are of natural colored stone, and such is normally the case in ancient finds, the surfaces of the tesserae will probably have a dull appearance when dry, so to intensify the color for pictures they have to be swabbed with a damp cloth and, as mentioned earlier, glycerin in the water will retard drying, though sometimes an oil is used rather than water (a practice not usually recommended in that the oil can discolor porous stones).

As with wall paintings some general views are needed to show the relationship of the decoration to the room or structure (if architecture is involved). Frequently this can best be accomplished by angle shots. But the entire mosaic should also be shot head-on for true scale if at all possible. Panels and details, naturally, are done in a like manner. Where the mosaic is a pavement the camera must be positioned exactly above the center point to produce an undistorted perspective. This means that it would probably be necessary to erect a scaffolding – unless the pavement is at the bottom of a trench and comparatively small in its dimensions (even here some planks across the trench will undoubtedly be

called for to get the head-on view). And scaffolding means trouble with shadows cast from itself, so the job is no simple one. To further compli-cate matters if the mosaic is too large for a single shot, it must be finished in sections where the procedure is to use white tape or string to enclose a rectangular part of the mosaic of the same proportion as the negative, and with this for a guide move the camera from one rectangle to the next for each subsequent shot – allowing for a bit of overlapping. In order that the rectangles will properly fit together for the finished print, the camera must maintain exactly the same distance above the mosaic for each picture in the series.

When the foregoing multiple shots are necessary the lighting can become a major headache, as the time required to make the series means that the illumination may change during the undertaking. The shadows of the tesserae will shift during the lengthy process causing a peculiar optical effect as a result. For either black and white or for color photo-graphy of mosaics, diffused light tends to be more equal, and less rough-ness will be apparent on the surface of the mosaic because of the lack of shadow thrown by the individual tesserae into the interstices. With panchromatic films a K2 (yellow) filter most closely approaches the colors as seen by the eye, and will in addition tend to darken any light blue stones that happen to be part of the color scheme and that would otherwise be likely to wash out. With color films the polarizing filter may eliminate any sheen or sky reflection off the surfaces of the tesserae if the correct angle can be achieved.

SCULPTURE

Sculpture is made in a great many materials, each creating its own problems and special needs photographically. Because of different characteristics consequent changes in lighting are needed.

Most sculpture of any size, whether relief, incised, or in-the-round, was made to be viewed in a vertical position. Therefore logically it is best photographed in a vertical position, a feat not always possible to attain when the piece lies at the bottom of an excavation. The most arduous part of the task is to find the lighting that will produce the best effect, and this is usually a matter of compromise. For example, shadow-less light, while helpful with very light colored materials such as alabaster or bleached wood or exceptionally dark surfaces like diorite, ebony, or bronze, is not beneficial for bringing out details, which are made most effective by shadows that emphasize the linear aspects. More-over, shadow is what brings out texture, an extremely significant factor

in sculptural photography, and at the same time shadow can obliterate detail and desaturate color if it spreads across too much of the surface.

The color of bronze varies with the mixture of alloys, and it is important for bronze, as for many other materials, to be photographed so as to show clearly a recognizable patina. The polarizing filter can often help bring this out by subduing surface reflections. Where the sculpture is set against architecture, as in a niche, a high-angle light is best in that what shadow there may be does not hopelessly obscure or confuse a large part of the surrounding wall and thus become distracting. Supplemental light or reflectors are generally helpful as fill-ins. The foregoing of course also applies to architectural sculpture (see Plate 7).

The cleaning of sculpture normally presents no great problems unless it is made of metals like silver or iron. Dirt is removed from the crevices with a knife, and a vigorous brushing and washing is normally suggested, perhaps even with soap.

SKELETONS

Human skeletons, either complete or in part, seldom offer any real difficulty for the photographer, the major chore (and it can be that) is a thorough cleaning. Original positioning of the skeleton is of first-rate importance to the archaeologist, so it must not be removed as a whole until adequately photographed. A northward pointing arrow should be included in burials, since orientation to a certain compass direction is often of religious significance. The state of preservation of the bones will be determined by age, type of soil in which they are found (if found in soil), and other usual factors that accelerate or retard decomposition. Bones may crumble when exposed to the air and need strengthening with a plastic compound, or they may be quite solid and capable of being scraped with a flat-bladed knife, perhaps even washed. At this point the photographer will need to rely upon expert help in the field, but, if there is a chance that the bones may not hold, it is unlikely that the site director would let anyone but an expert in this specialized area attempt to recover and clean the bones. In most instances where the bones are not individually removed for cleaning because of their fragile condition, the dirt around them should be undercut as much as possible (see Plate 10). Washed bones must be dry for photographing, as they are whiter that way. If the bones are brownish, an A (red) filter is in order for pan films; if they are yellowish-brown, a G (orange) filter is the one. With bones imbedded in chalk or other white soils, one might have to make the bones darker rather than lighter, and this is accomplished with a B

E

(green) filter. When color films are employed there is less difficulty distinguishing the bones from their surroundings.

Several angle shots can be made, but the most significant one is from directly above. Besides the complete skeleton, details of unusual aspects like broken bones, deformities, diseased conditions, jewelry worn or buried with the deceased, and perhaps his weapons, bowls for food, etc., could be useful.

Chapter 3
Photography in the Site Studio

Taking pictures of the site with all of its details may seem to the average person the most important and certainly the most glamorous aspect of archaeological photography; it may be the latter if there really is any glamor, but pictures made at the site studio will constitute an equally important part, possibly more film being shot indoors than out, as nearly each item found will be photographed, often from several angles. Perhaps the exception is sherds of a nondescript variety, but all else will receive careful scrutiny by the camera's eye. Most of these photos will end up as mere record shots, though a minority will be used for publication and lectures. If the pictures were all for record purposes only, one could without hesitation get along with a 35-mm reflex camera to do the whole job. However, since many photographers (and photo-engravers) prefer a larger size negative for pictures to be reproduced in magazines, books, reports, etc., the 35-mm miniature is often relegated to second place – or none. In recent years, though, more and more pictures, even color pictures for plates, are being produced on these small cameras and accepted without question for publication. What camera to use? Does one take pictures of all things on a larger size, or some on larger, some on smaller – or does one use only a 35? The last word may in fact not be the photographer's, for the director may veto his choice – or the director may leave it entirely to the discretion of the photographer, knowing that the latter has probably had enough experience to make a competent judgment. When the photographer decides to do the majority of studio pictures with the small camera, leaving only the most important things to a larger camera, a quandary still persists: which to take on what camera, for which is important? The director may have some suggestions, but the chances are that he will not always be sure what is important and what is needed for publication, because unless it is near the end of the season many things will yet remain to be unearthed and photographed, some probably pre-empting the significance of things previously found and recorded on film. There is no satisfactory solution unless someone makes the decision that film cost is too great for the large size exclusively, or that film cost is to be disregarded (wishful thinking!) and all be on the larger size. This is a policy matter and it

should be settled before the expedition starts, so that the proper amounts of films will be on hand. In the last analysis it is not a question of something or nothing, for small negatives can be used, though as noted in the preceding chapter there are some limitations – but in fairness also some advantages.

The foregoing is one possible course of action, but another is that the director may want the majority of studio photographing done back at home base where greater control of shooting is probably possible, doing only those things at the site studio which are not to be removed from the country, or which seem so fragile as to be in danger of damage during shipment. However, most directors want at least a quick shot of everything of any consequence, merely as a safeguard against unforeseen disasters. But, after all, a greater amount of time ordinarily is available at home, and studio work is one of the most exacting and lengthy types of archaeological photography, whether on an excavation or in a museum, so the photographer's time in the field might be more efficiently used in other ways. Again this is a policy matter and should be clear beforehand. Moreover, it can vary from site to site, depending upon the number and nature of the finds and excavation.

If there is no electricity and all photographing has to be done with daylight, this automatically limits the amount and kind of studio work that can be accomplished. In fact an outdoor studio of a kind may need to be devised – or a method of directing skylight and sunlight into a room (see section on Reflectors in this chapter, p. 66).

THE STUDIO

At least part of a room is needed where there is space for: 1. storing camera equipment; and 2. close-up photography of objects found, maps, etc. Actually such a place might turn out to be the living quarters, but most probably it will be the workroom where small items dug up are classified and stored. In any event the photographer must have some control over the light, both artificial and any daylight entering. Hopefully there will be electrical outlets for plugging in lamps, and such outlets and indeed the complete wiring system should be checked to see whether they will safely carry the wattage requirements (at least 1,500 watts). Lacking this, one or more cables out the window to a power line, generator, or other electrical source will have to do. A table and a means

of propping up backgrounds are the only further large requirements (not counting the camera equipment).

Preferably the camera equipment should be kept in a cabinet of some description where it cannot be handled by everyone who happens to enter the room. And in humid climates such a cabinet will need to be properly ventilated by means of an air conditioner or at the very least some burning bulbs to keep the air dry and circulating. Further information about such needs can be found in the Kodak pamphlet on *Tropical Photography* which has been referred to previously. A cabinet built to specifications may be worth shipping from home, with a crate built around it and the inside used for regular packing purposes.

CAMERAS

When there is money for it and the volume of work demands it, a separate view camera and a 35-mm reflex would be desirable for studio work. The 35 could be the same as used for outdoor shots, but it is well to have an extra 4×5-in. camera for the studio alone – assuming a big camera is used at all. Then if something happens to the main field camera, there is a satisfactory substitute available. However, the principle reason for the studio view camera is that the photographer may get a complicated set-up already to shoot and an urgent call from the field comes: 'Please hurry and bring the camera!' Then time is wasted taking down and setting up the camera once again. Of course, photographers have gotten along with a single camera and one tripod many times, but today's photography, especially if any color is taken, is more time-consuming and demanding than formerly, and any method of saving some of it is helpful and desirable. With this second camera a single lens (the normal-angle) will do quite nicely, supplemental plus lenses providing for close-up shots and a minus lens for long ones (providing the camera has a bellows).

TRIPOD

If one is going to have a camera reserved for studio purposes only, the system breaks down unless there is likewise a separate tripod for the studio. To make a portable tripod more stable and keep it from sliding on the floor, braces can be devised (see fig. 2, p. 26).

Pictures will be taken horizontally and vertically, and a height adjustment through an elevating center post is necessary, else the photographer will waste an inordinate amount of time trying to shorten or lengthen the tripod legs. So a good tripod with a suitable pan head that tilts in the two opposing directions is recommended. As indicated earlier a universal ball joint can be an adequate substitute for an all-directional tilting pan head if the camera is not too heavy, but ball sockets invariably allow a heavy camera to slip out of position and make minor adjustments difficult.

However, if a 35-mm range-finder camera is used, a long lens in a short mount attached to a reflex housing permits the attached camera to be easily swung from horizontal to vertical or some intermediate position without adjusting the tripod. This is also true for close-ups where the normal lens can be attached to some makes of bellows extension on 35-mm reflex cameras.

In an area where vases without feet are likely to be found, metal tripod stands upon which to rest such vases should be available.

FILMS

For black and white photography the pan films used outdoors do nicely for most indoor purposes, though when it comes to copying maps, charts, drawings, and such other things, one cannot very well ignore the useful value of an additional type or two (see later section on Copying, p. 81). Various filters can be used as for outdoors, except that an X1 filter replaces the K2.

The film materials for color photography indoors necessarily have a different color balance than do those suitable for outdoor work, although nearly all of these films also can be used outdoors with appropriate filters (again refer to the *Kodak Master Photoguide*). And like outdoor color films there are two general types: negative–positive and reversal.

Polacolor (with the proper filters) can be used at ASA 12 with studio lamps or flood if shutter speeds of less than $\frac{1}{10}$ second are possible. The 80B + CC20B filters are necessary.

TABLE

A rigid and level surface, preferably a sturdy table, is needed upon which objects to be photographed can be placed with reasonable

assurance that they will not be rocked over – or worse, off and onto the floor! The dimensions of the top should be not less than 30 × 48 in.; height from the floor can be standard table height (30 in.). At times several levels, perhaps as many as three, will be required for groupings of objects, so some step-like material approximately 6–8 in. high and deep can be improvised, and if these or the table are unsightly and no paint is available, they can be covered with bristol board or cardboard cut to size, or draped with a fabric.

STUDIO LAMPS

At least two studio lamps will be used at one time, often more, so that many lamp sockets with reflectors capable of holding the 500-W size bulbs are needed if electricity is available (with no electricity at the studio, sunlight and reflectors are resorted to as described in a following section, p. 66). The lamp sockets should have clamps which can be attached to telescopic stands or handy pieces of furniture that may be nearby.

While sunlight might be a means of getting by for black and white photos in a pinch, it is seldom satisfactory for color work in the studio. Moreover, in either case any volume of work will soon turn up a backlog of pictures if a reasonably standard and dependable lighting set-up is not to be had. The recommended lamps are 3,200°K studio type (General Electric: ECT PH/500PS25/5) rather than the 3,400°K photofloods (General Electric: EBV No. 2), because for color photography the color balance of the former does not greatly shift as the bulbs age, and also the rated life of the former is around 60 hours as compared to about 6 hours of the latter. Both use 115–120 volts, though the output in lumens of the former is slightly less.

Fluorescent tubes are not recommended for color photography, as they require heavy filtration, lacking as they are in certain wavelengths of light. Even the best filtration will not produce true color.

SPOTLIGHTS

Two or more spots are particularly helpful for concentrating light on small objects (coins, jewelry, etc.) and for projecting directional light across a textured surface to bring out its characteristic roughness (see

later discussion on Textural lighting, p. 75). The spots can use the same type of stands mentioned in the foregoing section on Studio lamps (p. 65), the base of the spots having suitable brackets that fit over the tops of the spots' uprights rather than having to be clamped to them; so stands should be purchased with this need in mind. Spots can be obtained that use less than the 500 watt lamps, for the concentrated effect upon a subject is that more light is present in the smaller area. It is well to note, however, that spots may be of a lower color balance than studio lamps, and when one is working in color a mixture of the two sources may create unwanted problems. Find out the Kelvin degree temperature rating of the spots before you leave home unless there is a color meter along – which is not a bad idea if much critical color work is envisaged. A light blue gel over the spotlight may be the answer.

REFLECTORS

Without electricity for lamps or spots one must improvise with reflectors, as flash or strobe are too uncertain in terms of predicted results for work in the studio. Two types of reflectors can be used singly or in combination: mirrors and matte surfaces (although some things like crumpled aluminum may be considered partly both). It is necessary to have the sun in such a position that the direct rays are angled off the surface of the mirror to the desired position, usually on to a matte reflector, which in turn reflects light to the subject. Incidentally a pane of glass or bright piece of tin make acceptable but slightly less efficient mirrors in an emergency. Of course, the sun does move, so much time is lost, when using sunlight in this way, in rearranging surfaces to get the light to fall on the object as wished. And just when the arrangement seems acceptable, presto! the sun has moved – or hides behind a cloud. Photography with this system becomes a real chore, and one cannot expect to turn out any real amount of work with it. Reflecting indirect sky light is another matter, for matte reflectors can be placed in one location and allowed to remain there, but the light level is considerably lower this way. And when color films are being used in this latter way the balance will be toward the bluish, and compensating filters will be needed to correct this condition.

Reflectors undoubtedly will still be needed when using studio lamps, and some method of clamping them to the light stands should be considered in advance. All told then about five or six upright stands

Plate 9.   Strobe for ancient underground aqueduct

Plate 10.   Inca artifact with light background

Plate 11. Inca artifact with black background

Plate 12.   Pueblo Indian skeleton in excavation

might be used at one time with lamps, spots, and reflectors. White bristol boards or cardboards can double as reflectors and as backgrounds; therefore they should be kept free of spotting marks and abrasions – a difficult thing to accomplish! Besides the matte surface of the bristol board, the latter covered with crinkled aluminum foil gives a slightly harsher light than the softer matte surface alone, the latter diffusing the light more than the aluminum. And white window shades are good for such purposes when new, but they yellow quickly with age.

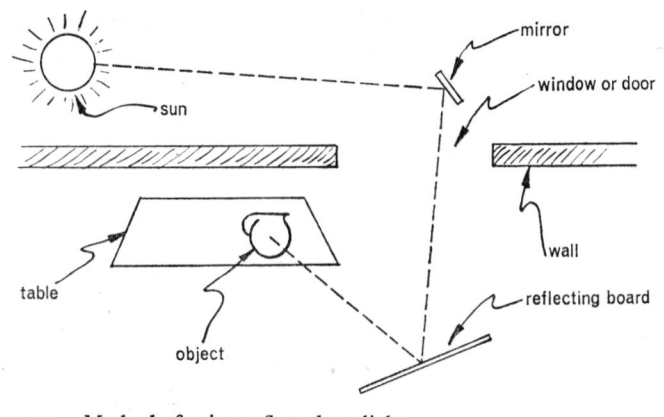

Figure 11.   Method of using reflected sunlight
   Note: one mirror is used to focus the sun's rays upon a reflecting board, which in turn reflects the light to the object.

Because in an emergency it may become necessary to improvise with mirrors and reflectors, the following system is offered (see fig. 11). The same set-up can be used in the field where objects are in shadow.

VERTICAL METHOD

Pictures in the studio with but a few exceptions are taken either vertically or essentially horizontally. In the first instance the camera points directly downward, either from a tripod (with a head that tilts 90°) or from a stand with an upright pole (on which a sliding bracket positions the camera). Both vertical methods will probably be used, but the latter is more convenient for small objects on the table or on a light box, a method that eliminates cast shadows which otherwise may be thrown across the object or background by the tripod's legs. This method is also

best for flat things like maps and drawings, or for copying pages in the field notebook (see later section on Copying, p. 81). The vertical method is one used for photographing objects normally seen in a flattened position when displayed, such as jewelry, coins, bits of bone, small pieces of pottery, etc., where they need to be contrasted against a shadowless background. The usual way of doing this is to elevate a piece of horizontally placed ground-glass (opal or flashed glass is optional) a half-dozen or so inches from the tabletop by means of blocks or legs, and then to place the object(s) on top of this. The glass should rest on the supports and not have the latter project above its surface, or shadows

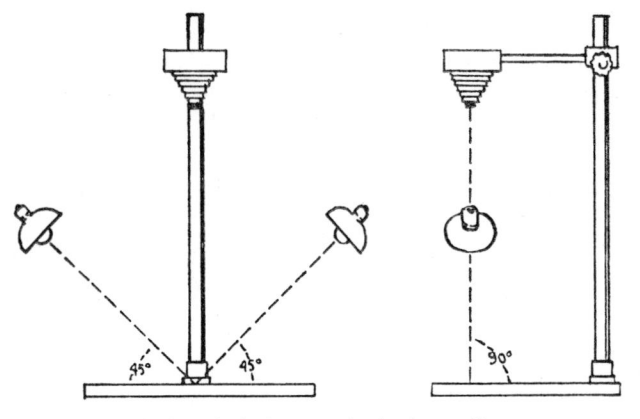

Figure 12. Method of vertical photography in the studio

of the supports can obscure some useable composing area. And ground-glass is preferred over clear glass to compose upon, for it eliminates the camera's reflection on the surface of the glass (if the ground side is uppermost). Plastic is optional, but is subject to scratching more easily. On the table top directly under the glass is positioned a background, usually a matte white cardboard or bristol board for black and white photos, but tints of appropriate colors can be selected for color filming. When objects are exceptionally light in tone it is often desirable to use a dark background of fabric material or velour paper, black for black and white pictures and deep shades of a harmonious color in the case of color work. For final publication in black and white it is advisable that all of the backgrounds be quite the same in tone, for when a group of photos appear on a page, a standard background usually appears preferable to a patchwork quilt effect. This then to a large degree may be the deciding factor. The same is not necessarily true of color, though

various color tones should perhaps be similar in value. Where a black background is used the glass mentioned above is unnecessary, for the black will absorb any shadows falling upon it (see Plate 11). The subject is usually illuminated by lights on opposite sides, the lamps placed at a 45° angle to the perpendicular (see fig. 12), an exception to this lighting being when the angle is increased toward the horizontal and one light is made stronger than the other by moving it closer for the purpose of accentuating textural details.

The same general procedure is carried out when a light box is available, and one can do it with the above materials if the object to be photographed is not too small, for a lamp must be placed directly under the object that rests upon the glass (the object must be large enough and opaque enough to hide the lamp under it). It is done in two steps: 1. with the light box dark and the object lit from the sides above, photograph the subject normally; and 2. without moving the camera, turn off the lights just used, and turn on the light box bulb under the object, double exposing the picture on the same film. For the second exposure try using one-half to two-thirds of the first exposure time. The second exposure will white out all shadows around the object and produce a completely white background (see Plate 10). This also could be done in color by interjecting a colored cellophane layer adhering to the underside of the ground-glass through which the light from the light box bulb would pass (or use a colored light bulb).

Vertical mounting of the camera eliminates much of the vibration that can otherwise occur horizontally, since with the assembly pointing downward, gravity makes any vibration act in the same direction as the optical axis rather than against it.

HORIZONTAL METHOD

Probably more often used and at the same time more difficult to execute because of the more complicated lighting problems, is the method where the camera on a tripod is aimed more or less horizontally at an object on the table. Instead of photographing flat subjects the photographer is now usually confronted with the necessity of showing depth and solidity. Groupings are most generally arranged on step-like platforms, the distribution being governed by one or more technical and/or aesthetic needs, a few of the possible major ones being: 1. objects to be placed in chronological order in terms of date or development; 2. larger items to

be positioned at the bottom, smaller at the top; 3. larger objects to be arranged near the center, smaller on either side; 4. articles to be placed so that their tops do not project above the next higher step; 5. types of the same or similar kind of things to be grouped on the same level; 6. a particular style order of objects to be placed; and 7. articles to be distributed according to color, texture, pattern, or some other characteristic. For single spherical objects like bowls and vases the camera position is somewhat above the objects to show the top opening as thin elipses (see Plates 14 and 15); where there are several tiers of objects the camera level should be just above the middle row of items (see fig. 13).

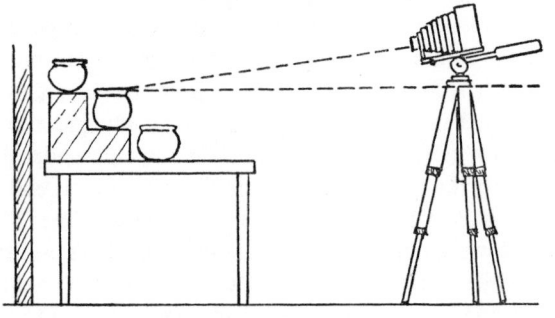

Figure 13.   Arrangement for three levels of objects
Note: the camera position is tilted slightly downward, so that an elipse of the middle bowl can be seen. Also the higher the camera on the tripod the sharper the angle, but the more flat the field becomes.

Getting too close to an object may seriously distort its profile, the method of overcoming this being to make use of a longer lens, or possibly with a minus supplemental lens in front of the normal one if a view or press camera is being used. Within reason the further back the camera's position, the more the lens sees the sides of round objects to get a truer contour (see fig. 14).

The question may arise in the photographer's mind as to which basic method of photography to use: vertical or horizontal. Alison Frantz notes in her article that, '90 per cent of the vases, terracottas and other objects on a town site will have lost their bases, their feet or their underpinnings generally, or if something remains for them to stand on, are otherwise so fragmentary that their original outlines, when seen in two dimensions, are distorted or confused'.[23] Failing any direction by the staff the photographer will have to make his own choice – or perhaps do it both ways. For the most part things that do not naturally stand and

are reasonably flat are best taken by the vertical method. When a foot or portion of the base is missing in a way to make the article unstable, a bit of Plasticine hidden in the rear will often furnish a suitable substitute foot. But a word of caution, for the Plasticine, being greasy, can stain the background surface if left too long, in which case a bit of wax paper judiciously placed underneath will save another background fatality. More expensive but non-greasy is a newer substance called 'Silly Putty'. Other things can be used such as pebbles, wire, plaster, and wood blocks, etc., and these could advantageously be collected and kept for the purpose.

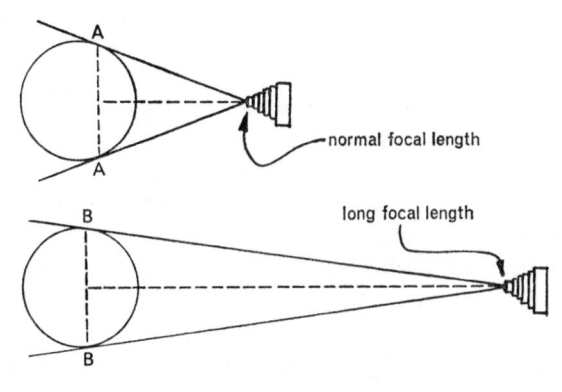

Figure 14. Method of achieving better perspective for contours of round objects
Note: line AA is shorter than line BB, indicating that less of the sides of the object in the top illustration is visible.

BACKGROUNDS

A large assortment of cardboard, bristol board, and fabric backgrounds should be a part of the paraphernalia of studio photography. White, light gray, and black surfaces will be used mainly for black and white photography, but colored backgrounds of light, medium, and dark values should be on hand for work in color. With the latter the photographer's aesthetic sense will need to rule as to what color(s) to employ, keeping in mind that contrast best shows the profile of objects.

Plain backgrounds almost without exception have been preferred to patterned ones, though in recent years publicity-type pictures in color have started a trend away from such surfaces, the danger being, however,

that any pattern will tend to overpower the subject and detract from its archaeological purpose. If we want to be frank about it, the simplicity of using a minimum number of plain backgrounds has had a lot to do with the use of them. But then there are so many objects to be photographed that one soon runs out of different backgrounds and patterned ones can thus become just as monotonous as plain ones. Then, as noted earlier, for publication where objects are to appear in two or more plates on a page, a standard background is usually preferable. Materials with an obvious texture are another matter – falling no doubt between the two extremes: plain and patterned. Realistically, patterned or textured backgrounds are probably best left to home base photography where the proper care and preparation of the fabrics and a wider selection of them is more feasible.

Almost invariably the end of the season and the last clean background never seem quite to coincide, the former arriving first, so an overestimation of the number of backgrounds needed is not a luxury. Nothing looks more horrible than a picture with a spotted background, and water spots and scrapes seem to appear for no reason – added by vexatious gremlins, no doubt! In commercial photography the background can be opaqued out, but this is taboo in archaeological photography, for '. . . no tampering is permitted, and the person using the photograph must be left in no doubt whether he is looking at the original outline or only an approximation of it'.[24] Since contours are most important in identification, any small deviation by the artist's brush in opaquing could result in a major classification error; no matter how expert the workman contours usually cannot be maintained with sufficient precision during opaquing. At any rate such a procedure can't be counted upon even if occasionally an artist could do a reasonably good job at eliminating the background without distorting the edges of the object.

Because light intensity decreases as the light sources are moved away, there is a direct effect upon the color or tone of a background depending upon where it is in relation to the subject. Well behind the subject, assuming there is no additional light source directed at the background alone, the latter will darken in color or tone. As a result it may be necessary to illuminate the background with supplemental lighting. In practice backgrounds are often moved some distance away from the subject to eliminate shadows, to throw the background out of focus if patterned or textured, or to get rid of slight blemishes on them.

One always has to be aware of extraneous reflected color in color

photography which can unnoticingly affect the subject's color, such as green walls or red curtains. These surfaces can effectively upset the color balance despite the stronger direct light from the lamps. And daylight entering can do the same; it can play particular havoc with color work done under tungsten light.

BASIC LIGHTING TECHNIQUES

Indoor lighting is normally made to simulate outdoor effect (there are some exceptions for special purposes). To achieve the foregoing, five considerations are usually necessary: 1. there should be one main source of light, and consequently one main set of shadows; 2. this main source should originate from above, preferably from a 40° to 60° angle to the vertical; 3. it should also be from an angle to the side, preferably the left; 4. the main light should not burn out detail in highlight areas; and 5. sufficient fill-in light is needed to discern some detail in the shadow areas. Exceptions to the preceding are sunless (shadowless) daylight that has its equivalent in the studio for photographing objects with shiny surfaces; and extra strong, low, and directional light which is frequently needed to detail texture.

The ratio of highlight to shadow should not exceed 4 to 1 in color and 6 to 1 in black and white for the best results in archaeological pictures, proportions easily calculated with an exposure meter. When the ratio becomes greater than these, shadow detail will start to disappear or highlight detail will wash out – or both (see fig. 15).

Figure 15. Lighting ratios
Method: multiply main-light-to-subject distance by fill-in factor; then place fill-in light at that distance.

Desired lighting ratio	1 to 1	2 to 1	3 to 1	4 to 1	5 to 1	6 to 1
distance factor for fill-in light	1 ½ stop	1.4 ⅔ stop	1.7 ⅔ stop	2 1 stop	2.2 1 stop	2.5 1⅓ stop

One method of photography for indoor subjects not used nearly enough by archaeological photographers is backlighting, a principle which emphasizes the solidity of form by separating it more clearly from the background. It is rather surprising that this method has been

employed so infrequently, since separating subject from background is one of the major objectives in archaeological photography. Actually it is simple enough to use a contrasting background to show a clear profile; and it is possible, although more difficult, to show up texture and details without sheen; but to combine the two is where all the skill of the expert is required. This skill is not easily come by, as it is achieved only after much experience; and it is also difficult to teach, each kind of subject having its own special problems that add to the multitude of complexities.

Figure 16.   Method of finding highlight placement

Lighting solutions considered best are those where the illumination is built up one light at a time, starting with the main source, until a satisfactory balance and clarity is established. Once the main light is positioned each successive light is adjusted as a fill-in to provide the light-to-dark ratio desired and the proper display of form, color, and detail is secured. Keep in mind the light-to-dark ratio ought to be somewhat less for color than for black and white photos, since the latitude of color films is proportionately less.

The positioning of the lamps used as fill-in lights to eliminate shadows is important; they are usually set at low angles. Not only is placement of the light sources important, but also the kind: studio or spot. Studio lights provide broad and diffuse shadow detail; a spotlight as a main source produces small specular highlights and sharp-edged shadows

with little detail in either if too strong, so generally speaking the studio-type lamps are preferred as the main source of light for most indoor archaeological photography.

Mirrors (like shaving mirrors with a slightly concave surface on one side) are handy in doubling as spots. They can even be masked off with black paper to reflect special shaped highlighted areas. These mirrors are particularly useful for illuminating small objects.

Highlight placement serves two purposes: 1. to assist in separating the planes of the object; and 2. to delineate the subject's surface. The principle of highlight creation is the placing of a small spotlight exactly in front of and in line with the axis of the camera's lens. Then by moving around, see where the best highlight effect shows up. By positioning the lamp where your head is at that moment the correct angle is established, since the angle of incidence equals the angle of reflection (see fig. 16).

TEXTURAL LIGHTING

Whether the surface is matte or glossy, rough or smooth, its characteristics will determine the type of lighting necessary to show the surface in the best possible manner. Keep in mind that a matte surface requires at least partly undiffused light, a rough-textured surface needs directional light, and a glossy surface is shown to best advantage with a completely diffused, non-directional light. When the surface is any combination of these then a combination of lightings is the only answer, but care must be taken that they do not cancel out one another or the objective will not be achieved. One has to decide which type should predominate. A diffused and non-directional light is obtained by several means: 1. employing an encircling material for small objects – a frame over which is draped or attached a white translucent substance like tissue paper, tracing paper, or a bed sheet, otherwise referred to as a tent, an improvised contraption not as familiar to photographers as it should be (see fig. 17), though care must be exercised that the metal frame (coat hanger wire?) does not throw a shadow; 2. using a translucent material in front of the lamps for larger objects (see fig. 18); 3. the use of bounce light – light from a studio lamp or spot directed against a cardboard, sheet, wall, or ceiling (for color photography one must make certain that the surface from which the light is to be bounced is white, else the reflected light will have the color of the surface and alter the color of the object being photographed); 4. polarize the light, a rather expensive

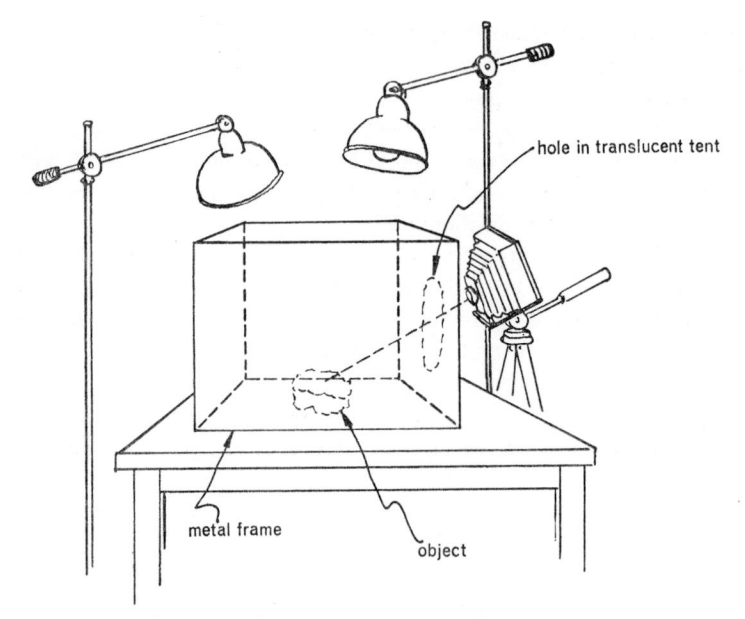

Figure 17. Tent for photographing small objects

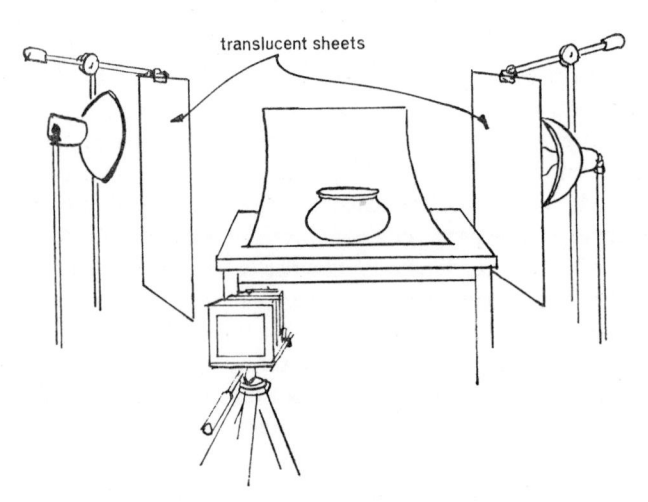

Figure 18. Translucent materials for photographing large objects

undertaking, since the polarizing screens, being large in diameter to cover the front ends of the lamp reflectors, are quite costly. Type II-B Pola-Screens (Kodak's designation) are placed over the front of the lamps' reflectors (one for each lamp), and after a Type I polarizing filter is placed over the lens, the latter is rotated until the desired effect is observed in the viewer. The screens and filter reduce the light by a considerable amount and long exposures are the norm. On pan and color films the polarizing factor for increased exposures is 3 to 4. Light illuminating the subject through the screens is metered in the usual manner with either an incident or reflected meter. A polarizing filter over the lens alone does some good, but one hundred per cent reduction in specular light is achieved only by filters on both camera and lamps.

Two other ways to help eliminate strong surface sheen or highlights from relatively smooth surfaces are: 1. spraying the surface with a substance known as matting spray (not to be used indiscriminately on all materials, particularly plastics – unlikely archaeological substances! – but the spray can be used on most metals and be wiped off easily); and 2. the use of what is known on the stage as liner, a cosmetic (Elizabeth Arden's Stage and Screen Make-up, No. 12) that can be brushed on and does a similar job as the matting spray. If both matte and shiny surfaces are present in the same picture, these last two solutions may be the only possible ones. All of the foregoing solutions subdue reflection quite nicely on glass too, although ancient glass is usually dull to begin with when found.

Notably important is the correct surface rendering of textiles, braided materials, and feathers, all of which require strong crosslighting to reveal their textures (see Plates 13 and 16).

A most helpful source of information in the general area of studio photography is Kodak's Publication No. o-16, *Studio Lighting for Product Photography.*

EXPOSURE

For general studio work exposure readings are probably best taken with an incident-type light meter, since seldom can one get a precise surface reading of reflected light from small or round objects. For very small objects the latter should be temporarily removed so that the meter can be placed in their exact spot.

As the camera is moved closer to the subject, the lens is moved further

from the film, the f/stop then being no longer a true indication of the lens's transmission power for extreme close-ups. Extra exposure is required and the simple formula to calculate this increase is as follows:

$$\frac{\text{lens-to-film}^2}{\text{focal length}^2} = \text{increase}$$

For example, using a camera with a 6-in. lens, when extended another 6 in. by racking out the bellows in securing the focus, the formula then in use is:

$$\frac{12^2}{6^2} = x \quad \frac{12 \times 12}{6 \times 6} = x \frac{144}{36} = x\,4 = x$$

It can be seen that four times as much exposure is required than the meter indicated. A simple dial calculator called, 'Effective Aperture Computer', made by Kodak, is available for this purpose, and it eliminates the actual mathematical computations. If instead of extending the lens, supplemental lenses are used, no increase in exposure is required; but if a minus lens is added for telephoto effect, an increase in exposure is indicated, as the bellows will be lengthened in the process.

When time exposures are necessary there is a reciprocity failure – the effective speed of the emulsion decreases, although such decreases are insignificant except for very lengthy or extremely brief exposures. The film manufacturer will supply the factors for reciprocity corrections if they are desired. In most cases the factor runs from one and a fraction at 1 second to about eight times at 90 seconds.

SCALES

Just as in the field, each picture should have an accompanying scale (except that the scale may be cropped from the final print for publication), and a number of small scales should be on hand – scales that the photographer can make himself with but little work. Though rulers can be purchased at stationery stores, they are generally unreadable in photos, so it is really better to manufacture them yourself. Provided in figure 19 are scales that may be photographed and then mounted on pieces of cardboard. Some are in inches, some in centimeters, and one in both. Refer to the chart in Appendix B (p. 122) for equivalencies. A number of scales should be made, for inevitably they get dirty or creased.

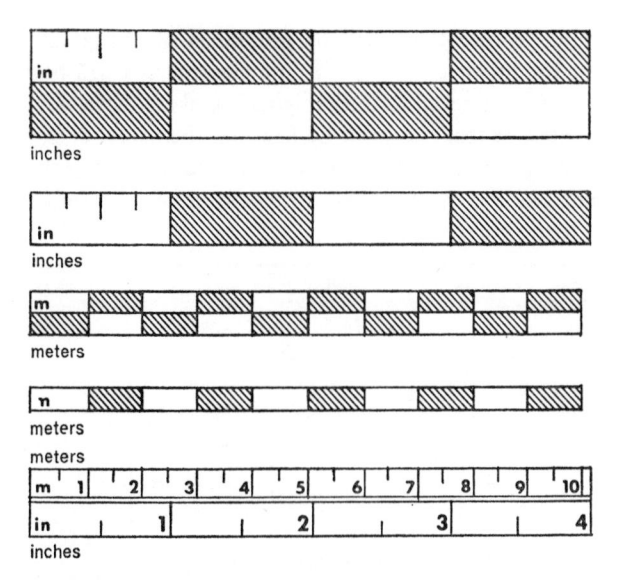

Figure 19.   Various scales for reproduction

Scales wrongly used are worse than none at all, and scales placed badly for close-ups can be completely misleading. For example, when a scale is positioned too far in front of an object, it is recorded on the film relatively much larger in proportion than the subject behind it that is being measured. Because no accurate measurements are really possible in perspective photographs, the use of scales has to be a compromise, placed as close to the object as space permits without concealing part of that object (scales placed that close cannot be cropped from the final print if this is desired). Flat subjects not in perspective are another matter, as measurements can be taken without difficulty on objects like coins (traditionally reproduced at 1:1), medallions, small bits of pottery, etc., the rule merely laid alongside to provide a true scale. When using roll film, many examples of coins, stamped amphora handles, etc., done on the same roll without changing the camera distance can have the scale established on the first frame only for the printer.

THE STUDIO NOTEBOOK

A similar notebook to that used in the field will be needed for the studio where pictures are taken of the many objects found, individually and/or

collectively. Because there will be groupings of objects at times, a record for the group as well as for the single items will be required, but this should be keyed to their original numbers, however. Here too a stamp could be made to print by hand on the pages, or pages could be mimeographed or printed on a press and glued together into a permanent binding. A suggested arrangement of such information is found in figure 20.

19 67	object (s)	light/reflectors	exposure	registry
OPAL COIN #1734 OBVERSE & REVERSE 7/16/67	2 LAMPS (3200) LFT ~ 24"LOW RT ~ 48" HI LAMPBLACK	CAMERA C 50mm LENS +3 SUP. POLAROID FIL. DOUBLE EXP, f/36 6 sec. EA. KODA II A	NEG #S165

Figure 20.   Page of photographer's studio notebook

Note: the *object(s)* column should include the type, number, and date; *light/ reflectors* refers to kind, number, distance, and direction of lights and reflectors, and any special treatment of object; the *exposure* column would include camera used, lens, supplemental lenses, filters, diaphram opening, shutter speed or time exposure, and film used; *registry* is negative (or positive) sequence number (S refers to studio to differentiate it from field or home base).

MATERIALS REQUIRING SPECIALIZED TREATMENT

A few materials need specialized treatment with the camera. Some of the same techniques used in photographing them outdoors may also be used for indoor work, so refer back to Chapter 2 where applicable.

POTTERY

Ancient ceramics, like old glass, are mostly found with dulled surfaces. To liven them up, especially for color photography, it is often feasible to dampen their exteriors when it is established that moisture will not destroy any design painted on them. Incised lines on pottery are occasionally difficult to see, notably in shadow areas, and a little white chalk rubbed on them with the finger and then lightly blown off can frequently make the markings clearer, for some of the chalk will remain caught in the lines.

When one photographs a piece of pottery an indication of its correct position relative to the orientation of the original whole object should be made if at all possible; it is desirable to be able to tell which is the top and which the bottom of the piece. 'Because of the wheel's revolution the potter's fingers leave minute scorings in the form of parallel grooves and ridges on the inner face of the fabric. If an isolated fragment from a wheel-thrown vase is so suspended that these scoring rings lie horizontal, the sherd will be oriented correctly in regard to the vase's vertical axis',[25] and the horizontal curvature may indicate top or bottom.

COINS
Due to the fact that it is commonly desirable that coins be shown in the same picture on both the obverse and reverse, this means a double exposure, and a black background is the usual method of doing this in the field, although a system of blocking off half the lens is not impossible. Some substance like lampblack paste rubbed over the surface of the coin and then mostly wiped off again so that only a trace remains in the deeper crevices and indentations will help to bring out the relief quality. Light should come from one direction and be low as in textural subjects, but just a bit diffused. A plaster cast can be made to show the opposite side of the coin. The technique is well detailed by Fraprie and Morris.[26]

GLASS
Transparent and translucent subjects, regardless of shape, are best illuminated with a single light placed behind the subjects and directed through them toward the camera, or the light directed at the background and bounced through the subjects; the latter is better for several objects photographed at the same time. In either case the light passing through them reveals both their form and translucent or transparent character more adequately than when the light is mainly from the front.

COPYING

The easiest and best way for copying in the studio when flat materials like books, maps, drawings, blueprints, etc., are involved is the vertical one described earlier in this chapter. With the copy lying flat (horizontally) there is no need for clips or pins that would otherwise be necessary to attach the material to a vertical surface if the horizontal method were employed. Placement of the lamps is critical; they must be positioned

at precisely equal distances and equal angles from the copy, else uneven lighting will occur (see fig. 11). Lamps placed lower or higher than a 45° angle often result in glare spots on the copy.

The kinds of black and white films suitable for the various types of copy work can be determined by test or experience. A good dealer can be of considerable help at this point. In black and white photography the developing and printing can do much to make more satisfactory results. For example, films for line work can be developed to a high contrast and printed on a high contrast paper.

Figure 21.   Special kinds of copying with filters for each

Material or condition	Filters and methods
paintings and half-tones in color	X-1 filter
pastel, pencil, crayon drawings in color	X-1 filter and possibly others place material under ground-glass, ground side down
stained photo or paper	filter of same but darker color than stain
blue prints	A filter
yellowed paper	A or G filter
ink faded to brown	C5 filter
creased or wrinkled paper	press under plate glass; use reflected light or polarizing filter

Special kinds of copying require filters when using black and white pan films (see fig. 21), and the filter factors will be found in the chart following (see fig. 22). Glass filters sometimes can slightly affect the focus at close distances, so focusing should be done with the filter(s) on the camera rather than attached after the focusing has already been done. A change in line voltage will also change the color balance of the lamps, a drop shifting the balance toward the red, a rise toward the blue. Copy work exposures are best achieved by reflection-type meters, a Kodak neutral gray test card used for continuous tone copy. If no gray card is available, a white paper can be substituted, the exposure index then

Plate 13. Peruvian textile lit from two directions

Plate 14. Pottery with directional lighting from above

Plate 15. Pottery with side and diffused light showing texture and linear detail

Plate 16.   Single light brings out textural detail of textile

being divided by five. Obvious caution must be that the meter does not read its own shadow as it is held over the copy. When an incident-type light meter is employed the hemispheric cone should be replaced with the flat disk-type light collector that usually comes with these meters.

Figure 22. Filter factors for indoor use

Filter	A	B	X-1	C5	G	K2
factor	4	8	2	10	2	1.5
f/stop	2	3	1	$3\frac{1}{3}$	1	$\frac{2}{3}$

Chapter 4
Special Kinds of Photography

In addition to the mere techniques of the following, some explanation of the nature of the problems themselves has been included in this section, as an understanding of these considerably aids an understanding of the techniques. Only those highly specialized techniques not generally applicable, such as periscopic photography done in Etruscan tombs, have been omitted from this section.

AERIAL PHOTOGRAPHY

This specialized method of archaeology undoubtedly will become more important in the future as known sites are exhausted through excavation and as archaeologists look about to find virgin areas, for aerial photography is no longer just a supplement to the traditional techniques of archaeology, but is often an avenue of discovery opened by no other method. Rhys Carpenter notes, 'in this connection aerial photographic reconnaissance should prove of the greatest service by scanning large areas with remarkably complete coverage of their surface and supplying pertinent information wholly inaccessible to the earthbound prospector'.[27] Moreover, 'with the help of such photography, it is possible to plot and map even the known ones [tombs, roads, etc.] very much more quickly than can be done on the ground'.[28]

In some locations this technique is notably unsuccessful, for Heitzer writes, 'we became fully convinced that aerial photography has nothing to offer as a means of locating archaeological sites in the Amazon area'.[29] But not far away the technique was eminently successful, as 'study of the air photos made [by the Peruvian Air Force] shows numerous archaeological sites in the Virú Valley [Peru], most of which were unreported'.[30]

Trees, grass, bushes, cultivated fields, sand wastes, etc., in air photographs all have different appearances in texture or tone. This applies to both black and white as well as color photography – even more so in the latter. Numerous instances have been well documented concerning the discovery and plotting of Roman roads, Etruscan tombs, and the like from aerial surveys.

Crop-marks, for instance, show up the conditions beneath ground level, reveal walls, ditches, and other shapes and information about ancient habitations, tombs, and boundaries. In Atkinson's book[31] a plate shows an aerial view of Foxley Farm near Eypsham, Oxford, with two kinds of crop marks plainly visible: 1. a field with green crops that indicate ditches in a darker tone because the roots of the crop have gone deeper into the soil and consequently received more nourishment (hence a color change from the air); and 2. another field with ripe crops where a somewhat taller growth occurred over former ditches, thus throwing a shadow that revealed the underground formations. In another plate[32] of a Roman Villa Site at Dichley, Oxford, again two types of crop-marks are seen: 1. light lines indicating the position of walls (crops got less moisture); and 2. dark lines showing ditches. Cottrell writes 'once the subsoil has been disturbed it can never be replaced exactly as it was before'.[33] While basically true this statement is somewhat misleading, for 'not everything, everywhere, will thus reveal itself to the aerial camera's eyes'.[34] And the author goes on to mention how drifting sand effectively blankets all underneath it in both arid deserts and along shorelands; agriculture too, for instance the planting of new vineyards, the spreading of thick layers of soil, and the introduction of irrigation systems, works against aerial photography as a good detection technique in archaeology.

These introductory remarks to aerial photography seemed necessary, since the photographer must recognize what he sees from the air when he sees it, or he may not really see it as he does not know what to look for. It does take a trained expert to read an air photograph and get all the required information from it necessary for its fullest use, as 'it is possible to misinterpret the black and white photographic record from overhead (much as a surgeon, it is said, must learn to read correctly the X-ray photograph, which cannot lie but may mislead)'.[36]

There are two basic kinds of aerial photographs for archaeological purposes: vertical and oblique; each does something better than the other, both being useful for specific jobs. The vertical method is normally employed for large-scale continuous mapping in which pictures are taken sequentially every so many seconds as the plane flies in a series of parallel lanes, while allowing some overlapping of views to provide, in the end, a mosaic map. This type of map: 1. gives a uniform definition of objects at any location on the surface; and 2. can be scaled, the scale depending upon the focal length of the lens and the height of the camera above the ground (known height of land above sea level is

subtracted from the plane's altimeter reading). The scale usually is stated as a representative fraction (RF) or as a ratio, the RF equaling the focal length (f) of the camera lens, divided by the height (H) of the camera above the ground. Thus:

$$RF = \frac{f}{H}$$

For example, a 2-in. focal length lens (normal lens of a miniature camera) at 2,000 ft above the ground will give an RF scale of 1/12,000 or 1:12,000.

The oblique method has two variations: high (usually showing the horizon) and low (aimed somewhat beneath the horizon) as illustrated in figure 23. Two disadvantages of the oblique method are: 1. definition

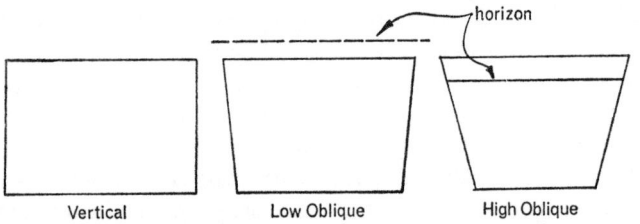

| Vertical | Low Oblique | High Oblique |

Figure 23. Vertical and oblique aerial photograph areas showing shape of earth's surface covered by each

Note: the rate of change in coverage of surface is greater in the high oblique than it is in the low.

loss with the distance; and 2. no scale possible (same as linear angular perspective). But the oblique has several advantages, the most important of which is its capacity for showing better physical characteristics of objects having a decided vertical dimension.

The camera for the vertical method is usually a special mapping camera designed for the purpose. On the other hand nearly all cameras can be used for the oblique method. Any negative will have to be enlarged, so even a miniature camera is highly useable, although most photographers would probably prefer at least a 4 × 5-in. negative size. The usual black and white film is a panchromatic base, but color adds much, as was found out in aerial reconnaissance photos for wartime Army and Air Force intelligence, although proper filters can improve the reading of black and white records. Infrared film is also used (see later section in this chapter on Infrared photography, p. 93).

Unlike the normal aerial mapping technique, which is done at midday to eliminate as many obscuring shadows as possible, archaeological aerial pictures are taken earlier or later, since shadows are of prime

significance in showing up uneven ground under which may be long-buried walls, etc. A high sun tends to give a flat appearance, but a low sun accentuates texture. And lighting seems more natural from what is known as the 11 o'clock position, the upper left.

Large scale mapping is seldom done under 7,500 ft, because turbulence of the lower air makes it difficult for the pilot to maintain a straight, level course necessary for accurate work. But for archaeological photographs when single areas are to be shot, lower altitudes are perfectly feasible and even desirable.

Since the direction of shadows changes with the sun's movement during the course of the day, pictures taken at different hours and then compared will frequently reveal features – ground irregularities, for example – that would be missed if only one picture was available. Filtering for black and white films is the K2 (yellow), which cuts a bit through light haze and produces a better differential of tones of areas normally green. Haze or polarizing filters can be used for color films.

Stereoscopic aerial views may add information like the aforementioned ground irregularities that often conceal burrows, earthworks, grave mounds, and other similar features of interest to the archaeologist.

Kodak publishes a handy *Aerial Exposure Computer* (Publication No. R-10), which has a Time-Motion Dial, an Exposure Dial, a Latitude Zone Map, and Solar Altitude Tables. This guide is invaluable for any extensive serious work in aerial photography.

The earliest method of aerial photography, and one still in use, is to suspend a camera under a tethered balloon. A recent note in *Archaeology*[37] explains its application at Sardis. They used a non-static spherical balloon 10 ft in diameter, made of cotton with a rubber-impregnated interior and an aluminum coating. Hydrogen was the gas which was used for inflation. The camera was attached under the balloon in an open tetrahedron frame made of aluminum tubing. The ground control line was attached to a corner of the frame to keep the camera from swinging and turning, and the shutter tripped by a long air tube and pneumatic bulb. They report that the height of the balloon was limited (about 50 meters) to the length of this tube.

PHOTOGRAMMETRY

A newly devised method by Julian Whittlesey of using a bipod camera support for vertical photography is described in a short but important

article in *Archaeology*.[38] This is a method of producing measurements from photographs by suspending a camera between two meeting poles in an inverted V formation (height about 6–10 meters). By swinging the poles along an axis with their pivot points stationary, a mosaic of shots can be obtained. When established reference points are used accurate horizontal dimensions can be read, and vertical dimensions can be computed by scale if a stereo camera is substituted.

UNDERWATER PHOTOGRAPHY

Interest is increasing in underwater photography, a field that was first extensively opened up by skin divers who, not being archaeologists, failed to comprehend certain values of scientific excavation. Hence few scientific approaches or records were attempted until archaeologists became interested in the spectacular finds from ancient ships that sunk with their valuable cargoes. But the pity of it is that the two, divers and archaeologists, have not gotten organized on any widely cooperative basis. There has been, however, an increasing degree of joint efforts. Once the problems are understood it is easy to realize why such co-operation has been minimal. Honor Frost has written: 'any excavation must be undertaken by a professional archaeologist, but no professional archaeologist can be a professional diver as well. With, at best, amateur status as a diver, the archaeologist will be at a disadvantage at marine levels. The solution must be a collaboration between the two profes-sions.'[39] Part of this statement could be questioned depending upon how one interprets the word professional. Certainly many experts are found as amateurs in most areas of endeavor. George Bass says: 'it is far easier to train scientists to dive than to train divers to be scientists'.[40] Miss Frost further goes on to say[41] that if such collaboration were to occur, a standard technique of underwater excavation could be evolved, and in the process a generation of young archaeologists might develop to carry out the work. 'No pilot excavation on these lines has as yet been carried to completion',[42] though there has been some limited collabora-tion to be sure.

Different from buried structures or objects on land, an object on the sea floor, such as a wreck 'undergoes a sea change before it becomes stabilized within the local geological environment'.[43] Perfectly recogniz-able things on land are often meaningless in underwater photos, and must be accompanied by drawings. For example, in a flat photo a sponge

growing on an amphora can look like a hole in it. Underwater marine growth flourishes as well on a rock, artifact, or concreations, and effectively camouflages shape and size and, if not too deep, color.

But there have been some few attempts at trying to use basically land archaeological methods to expose wrecks. Miss Frost discusses[44] how Dr Roghi excavated a Roman shipwreck at Spargi, noting that he divided the surface of the wreck in 2-meter squares by means of stretched tapes. Three meters above the center of each squared off section he took a photo. Plans could be drawn from these photographs. But what sounds so simple was amazingly difficult – as is everything underwater for man. As an example, he could not continue the process of excavation in depth, once the top layer had been raised, until the water had cleared enough for viewing. Because of water resistance all movements are both clumsy and tiring, and the time a diver can remain submerged is quite limited (without a pressure chamber).

Four magazine articles are of interest in telling (and showing in pictures) about underwater archaeological methods, as well as items recovered. The earliest article[45] was in January 1954 and gives an account of the discovery of an ancient Greek ship that sank about 230 B.C. off the Marseille coast at a depth of 140 ft. TV cameras were also used to get pictures of this operation. The second article[46] appeared in the summer of 1961 and described a drafting frame with provision for mounting a camera to take vertical pictures. A third article[47] was published in May 1962 and the author discussed among other things the dangerous currents that harassed the team from the University of Pennsylvania under the direction of George Bass as they dove for a Bronze Age ship off Cape Gelidonya, Turkey. Divers had to struggle in lowering themselves 90 ft down the shot line. Limestone deposits covered all, as they do everything in the Mediterranean, and formed a coating of almost concrete-like hardness. The fourth article[48] of January 1963, concerned another wreck off the Turkish coast in which iron scaffolding was erected over the wreck in the form of a grid that permitted archaeologists to plot the vessel's size and type with accuracy. In addition a mapping frame was used which resembled a square steel spring cot, a frame with wires at right angles. The description by Bass is as follows: 'First we placed a scaffolding of pipe and angle iron over the entire wreck. . . . Then we constructed two movable towers, each 13 feet high, to hold our cameras in fixed focus. . . . We could plot planks and nail holes exactly to the centimeter. The time-consuming business of drawing underwater was practically eliminated.'[49]

Visibility varies greatly from day to day and from place to place under the surface. Blue water is the clearest and has the highest visibility. The particular colors are produced by the scattering of the light by water molecules and tiny suspended particles. Green water is less clear and the coloring comes from particles of yellow pigment derived from plant life in the sea. Additional colors are the result of other particles in suspension. Variations also occur because of: 1. turbidity in the form of sedimentary matter; 2. temperature changes; 3. type of bottom (rocky, sandy, muddy, etc.); 4. exposure to waves (including storms) that diffuse the light; 5. tidal action; and 6. time of day (less reflection from surface downward if the sun is directly overhead). To complicate matters turbid water may overlie comparatively clear water or vice versa, the worst turbidity being found in harbors and estuaries. Wind conditions are of importance, since winds blowing toward land cause wave action that can stir up bottom sediment. At the edge of large land masses winds are onshore at midday and static or offshore at other times, so early morning and late afternoon therefore are often good times for photography, as they are apt to be times of less turbidity. But then the lighting is poor if one is depending upon natural light – and it is poor even at best. Illumination is usually so inadequate underwater that large lens openings and auxiliary lights are normally required. Because of necessarily large apertures for the lens, close objects require critical focusing, and the wide-angle lens, which has a great depth of field, is frequently called upon for the best results. Unfortunately the wide-angle lenses available are not usually as fast as those of normal focal length.

Refraction is another problem, as the refraction of light magnifies everything underwater; distances appear only three-quarters of their actual distance and objects appear one-quarter larger (index refraction of water is 1.333). For example, an area of a certain width photographed at a distance of 9 ft on land requires 12 ft under water. 100 ft is exceptional visibility, and most pictures are made within 10–30 ft.

Color below 10 ft will lack some amount of red and yellow if natural light is employed. Beneath 30–40 ft only blue remains – until it disappears finally with all light. This is why many available light pictures taken at some depth are seen all in monochrome of blues, or when artificial light is used the distance not penetrated by the light appears bluish. Naturally at any depth proper artificial lighting will reveal close to true color of nearby objects.

When diving is to be done below 10 ft (with one exception) a pressure-proof watertight case around the camera must be used. At 10 ft the

pressure would be approximately 200 lb on even a small camera, and this pressure increases sharply as one descends and as the size of the camera increases. Pressure then is an important consideration. Watertight cases are now commercially available, or they can be engineered to specifications with watertight packing glands for controls projecting through the cases and gaskets to seal the lids. These latter present particular problems, as do the openings through which the photographs are made, the latter normally of glass (quartz for deep sea equipment); plastic is not abrasive-resistant enough for such use. The smaller the camera, the smaller the housing that is needed, so miniature cameras find ready acceptance for underwater photography. Better for focusing however are the $2\frac{1}{4}$-in. single-lens reflex cameras, and they are not much larger. The exception mentioned previously is the Nikonos, an amphibious all-weather 35-mm camera that takes pictures underwater without a housing, being hermetically sealed, salt water resistant, able to withstand water pressure to 160 ft down, and having a 35-mm f/2.5 lens. Housings are made for larger cameras such as the $2\frac{1}{4}$-in. double-lens reflex cameras and even movie cameras.

Requirements for a camera to be placed in a watertight housing are: 1. it must have roll film; 2. be a box type (not bellows) so that the lens focuses in a helical rotating or sliding mount; 3. be rugged and shock-resistant; 4. be sychronized for flash and strobe; and 5. have the film transport, shutter cock, diaphram opening, shutter speed control, and release, all adaptable to auxiliary controls operating through a watertight case. In addition it is desirable to have interchangeable lenses. Cameras with an automatic exposure are not generally suitable, as compensation has to be made for underwater exposures. Some cameras have automative spring-driven or motor-driven film advance as a further useful refinement. The reflex camera seems advantageous over a range-finder type, as no correction for refraction is necessary, the view seen on the ground-glass being the one recorded on the film, and this makes for improved composition and focus.

Condensation within a watertight housing can be a vexing problem, for the latter is normally assembled in the warmer air on the surface, while the coolness of the water in which it is submerged causes droplets to form on the inside of the cold surface of the housing lens To overcome this condition coarse-grained silica gel, a dehydration chemical, is used within the casing. Heating of this desiccating agent in an oven restores its capacity to absorb water again after it has become saturated.

Since it is difficult to estimate distances under water, a weighted

measuring pole with footage marks may be employed; and scale sticks are as necessary for underwater archaeological pictures as for ones on land, but a non-corrosive metal should properly be used. Notes or drawings need to be made under water. The simplest material to use is plastic 'paper', sheets of frosted flexible plastic on which ordinary pencils can be used for drawings; or a grease pencil will allow for hastily scribbled notes on pieces of rigid clear plastic.

Exposure meters (both basic types) can be read in error and indicate less exposure than is actually necessary, resulting in underexposure. On the one hand the incident meter reads the light traveling through only half of the water (surface-to-meter, not surface-to-subject-to-meter). On the other hand the reflection meter at the subject does not account for loss of light between subject and camera; and at the camera it does not read the subject but reads the horizontal scattering of light. Obtaining the correct exposure is mostly a matter of experience. Most photographers prefer to use the reflection-type meter, taking a reading halfway to the subject and turning the meter slightly down to avoid the bright surface of the water above.

In most cases there will be a need for auxiliary lighting equipment. Photofloods or electronic flash units must be properly designed for safety, as electrical shock is possible with improperly designed or carelessly used lights. In this respect they are more dangerous in salt water than in fresh.

R40 photofloods are the best of the lamps, as they contain a built-in reflector (40 refers to the degree angle of the beam, which approximately equals that of the camera's normal lens). If a wide-angle lens is on the camera several lamps must be used to cover the whole area. When handling electrical equipment under the surface the preference is for direct current – which usually means batteries. If alternating current is used, the diver must wear a swim suit that completely insulates him from contact directly with the water. When long electric lines are employed a drop in voltage can be expected, and this causes a decrease in color temperature of the lamps – a shift toward the red, not a serious fault, for a loss in this portion of the spectrum occurs anyway. Floods must be turned on after they are submerged and not before, else they will explode as they enter the cold water.

Because the electronic strobe uses extremely high voltage it involves considerable danger in its operation. Complete insulation by a waterproof and pressure-proof housing must be the rule. Such equipment is available commercially.

Clear flash bulbs, because they give off more red light, are a good choice if the circuits are well insulated. At a distance of 6 ft nearly 25 per cent of the red in a flash bulb will be absorbed by the water. The bulb and socket can be in contact with the water, so it is possible to change bulbs on location. Naturally the battery case and leads to the camera and bulb socket must be watertight. At considerable depths two or three flash bulbs may be needed to penetrate enough distance. There is a limit to the depths a flash bulb can be used when not in a pressure case, for it will of course collapse under water pressure at a certain point, depending upon the type, shape, and size of the bulb. The smaller the bulb, the better it can withstand such pressure, so multiple smaller bulbs are often more satisfactory than one large bulb. Slave units (either bulb or strobe) in separate housings can be extremely useful, for they can be arranged at some distance from the camera.

To calculate exposure for floods, flash bulbs, or strobe, the distance between light and subject needs to be decreased by at least half. This is for clear water; for turbid water a further increase in exposure or other compensating changes are necessary. In fact it is advisable to make several shots and bracket the exposure ($\frac{1}{2}$ to 1 stop on either side of the calculated exposure).

If black and white films are used, only the pan type is recommended, and possibly a K2 (yellow) filter should be employed to decrease the excessive blue that can alter the appearance of the tones.

Several American companies supply commercially various kinds of underwater photographic equipment. These are noted in another helpful booklet published by Kodak, *Underwater Photography with Black-and-White and Color Films*, Sales Service Pamphlet No. C-25. It also mentions several books that may be useful for the more technical aspects of diving.

INFRARED PHOTOGRAPHY

The 'light' waves of the infrared part of the spectrum are invisible to the human eye, yet they can be recorded on film and the results seen on that film or prints made from it. But the quantity of infrared radiation emitted from a particular surface cannot presently be predicted with certainty, test exposures being required – or possibly by experience one can achieve a close estimate. No meter is now available to measure this

radiation, although such a one is certainly feasible if there was a demand for its manufacture.

Infrared film can assist the archaeologist in spotting certain things not usually recorded well (if at all) on other types of films. In comparison pictures taken of strata of earth, for example, the print of the infrared picture often shows up some characteristics to which the pan film is totally blind. J. Beuttner-Jannaech illustrates this with pictures in an article where he also said: 'not only did features in the profiles show up clearly in the prints, but some appeared which were not visible in prints made with panchromatic film and which were not apparent to the eye'.[50] Stratifications are frequently more clearly defined with infrared.

In conjunction with aerial photography infrared is quite useful in enhancing the contrast of the terrain. Shadows, for instance, show up as dark areas, but often reveal much detail besides; cool objects appear dark, warm objects appear light; hence green vegetation looks very whitish, while water is blackish. In oblique aerial shots great clarity of distant objects and detail is obtained, for the film effectively pierces fog and haze – even darkness. Hammond notes that 'the application of this technique [infrared] for site photography is of possible value in terms of detecting vegetation changes over certain underground remains.'[51]

In restorations or examination of paintings and certain other works of art, infrared has proved its usefulness, and conceivably the secrets of some ancient materials, such as manuscripts and scrolls, might be brought to light if they were subjected to this technique.

Standard infrared film requires an A (red) filter, a typical exposure of an air photo being $\frac{1}{100}$ second at f/5.6 with Kodak's sheet film type or f/8 with miniature film. Ground views and close-ups need more exposure respectively. Development is by one of four possible popular formulas.

Because of their longer wavelength infrared waves do not focus through camera lenses to the same point as visible light waves; rather there is a slight increase in focal length necessary. The smallest lens openings consistent with the shutter speed should therefore be used to assure best definition. Many lenses have a special marking for this purpose, but others do not, so tests will then need to be run.

If infrared photography is contemplated, the acquisition of another Kodak booklet is recommended: *Infrared and Ultraviolet Photography*, Publication No. M-3.

Polaroid infrared film is now available and Kodak has introduced an Ektachrome infrared (a combination of color film and infrared film

which produces a false color but one often considerably more helpful for specific colors, especially in aerial work). This latter film differs from ordinary color film by having its three sensitized layers sensitive to green, red, and infrared radiation rather than the usual blue, green, and red wavelengths. A yellow filter (G or K2) is used. Focusing is in the normal manner, but small apertures are recommended.

ULTRAVIOLET PHOTOGRAPHY

Outside the study of old manuscripts and paintings, ultraviolet photography has been little investigated as a tool for the archaeologist. Undoubtedly the future will find many significant uses for it in the examination of paints on ancient pottery and the like.

This technique requires no different photographic equipment except certain ultraviolet lamps and appropriate filters for the lamps. Either pan or color films are used, and processing is in the usual manner. The aforementioned booklet by Kodak is a helpful guide.

Basically there are two kinds of UV lamp as sources of radiation: long and short-wave. Some things fluoresce when excited by one wavelength, some by the other, and some by both. Films can record either reflected light or the actual radiation of the fluorescent materials or both.

One variation is to dust the object with fluorescent or phosphorescent powder to bring out certain details. Little apparently has been done in this area.

X-RAY PHOTOGRAPHY

Not available for general field use as yet, X-ray photography holds perhaps more promise than the two previously mentioned techniques for the archaeologist. Hammond writes [52] that X-ray photography helps to determine the shapes of corroded objects in metal, methods of construction, contents of core-cast sculptures, and similar data, and adds that the information gained from its use is valuable for reconstruction purposes. All of us have seen X-ray pictures of mummies taken to show the jewelry inside the wrappings. Brothwell and Higgs [53] included in their book a paper on the use of X-ray fluorescence in ancient glass as a

means of typing. The future will see many diverse procedures for archaeological purposes with this technique, and portable units are in the process of development. Within a few years X-rays surely will be readily available in the field, the only serious obstacle being cost.

SODIUM VAPOR AND MERCURY VAPOR PHOTOGRAPHY

Some experiments have been made with these light sources and combinations of these and others, mostly for the purpose of making incised lines and edges clearer on stone and bone artifacts. However, it is doubtful whether the involved techniques result in a sufficiently significant advantage over other methods for the archaeologist.

The bibliography lists a booklet by M. Déribéré that is the best source of information on experiments in this field. Page 65 of this booklet illustrates a superimposed picture of a fourth-century Carthaginian stele taken on black and white pan film with a fluorographic negative to create somewhat clearer detail. Something of the same nature can also be done with sodium and mercury exposures.

PHOTOMICROGRAPHY

In the aforementioned book[54] another paper describes microscopic identification of ancient metals. One of the latest interests is a study of obsidian hydration that requires microscopic examination. Any magnified small object falls into the category of micrography, and requests for photos of this kind for record or publication purposes are increasing, although the technique is perhaps more suitably practised in permanent installations where controlled conditions exist. Still it can be attempted in the field with considerable success. The scope of things that are of interest to the archaeologist runs the gamut from pollen to crystals, thread to bark, blood to clay, and pictures of minute differences of such materials are often extremely important to clear identification of the age and place of manufacture of buried objects.

This photographic process is actually quite simple; all that is required is an attachment to couple a reflex camera to the microscope. One useful

camera for photomicrography is the Bessler Topcon with a behind-the-lens meter that measures precisely the light coming through the microscope to which it is attached – a tremendous advantage in getting good exposures without wasting film (and time). Illumination is by lamp either through the substance photographed or reflected from it. In the latter case a very strong light source is required, and electronic strobe is useful in this regard. Kodak's *Techniques of Microphotography* (Publication No. P-52) and *Photography through the Microscope* (Publication No. P-2) are suggested reading.

In addition to pan and color films being used with standard lighting procedures just mentioned, both polarized and ultraviolet sources of light are possible, though again little has been done with the latter.

MOTION PICTURES

Some things have already been mentioned in previous chapters concerning this technique, and filming methods, sequences, ways to cut from one scene to another, laps, dissolves, zooms, warnings about excessive panning, etc. – all these and others can be found in many good books on motion picture production, and these should be consulted.

Motion pictures of an archaeological nature are taken primarily for one of two reasons, perhaps both: 1. public relations; and 2. lecture and/or instruction. As earlier stated some commercial use could conceivably be made of the film too, but this is not really a true archaeological intention.

It should be self-evident that motion pictures are *moving* pictures; nothing is more deadly on the screen than non-moving motion pictures – in any field. Pictures at the site must have people in them, people doing things – recognizable things and things that make sense (perhaps assisted by good narrative commentary). Interest should be generated as the film progresses, and that interest needs to be maintained throughout by a story-like procedure, for a film should never be a hit or miss kind of production – growing like Topsy by grabbing a few feet every now and then between still shots on Sundays. A pre-planned script is necessary, although it can be modified as situations arise, but even then one should weave the new situations into the basic script if possible rather than have to spend additional time in the field working on a major revision. Not only motion, but continuity, variety, and aesthetic appeal are basic requirements. The picture may well begin before the expedition leaves

by showing preparation, then including shots of the trip, customs at the port of entry, local color, arrival at the site, hiring natives, etc.

All of the fundamental techniques of still photography can be used in motion pictures (except flash or strobe for illumination). There is even a comparatively inexpensive portable floodlight on the market with batteries that can be charged in about an hour if electricity is available.

Kodachrome II Daylight film (or equivalent manufacture) will probably be used, but Type A film with an 85 filter at 24 fps (sound speed; for sound will need to be added later even if it is not recorded while filming) can be used if one wants to stay with just one film for both indoors and out – unless a blue filter is used over the flood, in which case outdoor film can be run in the camera throughout. However, one usually wants as bright a flood as possible, and the blue filter would cut down on the light level somewhat.

It has been said that a good motion picture is really made in the cutting room (by editing), but don't take this too literally, since, when there is not good footage to begin with, no amount of editorial slicing can produce satisfactory results.

MUSEUM PHOTOGRAPHY

The photographer is frequently called upon to go to a local museum and make copies of material or do original photographs of exhibits for comparative or informational reasons. This task can probably best be accomplished with a 35-mm camera, and when the possibility is foreseen a faster film than usual would be advisable, whether in black and white or color, as the light levels of most museums are quite low as compared with studio lighting. This applies to copying flat material in libraries as well as displayed objects in glass cases. Good pictures of articles in cases are frequently impossible because of surface reflections on the glass; here a polarizing filter might help if a tripod is used and the angle to the glass is from 32° to 37°. Without special lighting set-ups, it is practically impossible to get accurate color in many museums, the reasons being: 1. the often hodge-podge assortment of types of lights; 2. a haphazard arrangement of the lights; and 3. the low light level. But the chances are better for the person with an archaeological team than if he were on his own, for the museum would ordinarily cooperate by removing the objects to a more suitable location for photographing – if the request was reasonable that is. A color meter is a considerable

advantage to attain the proper color balance, but objects lighted by fluorescent lamps cannot be properly filtered.

To make note of things photographed in other locations, especially in museums, another notebook will be needed – not a complicated one, but merely a sequence record of each exposure and important accompanying data about the objects in that particular picture. Probably another spiral-bound variety is satisfactory, and the information in it can be transferred later to a more permanent form if desired.

Chapter 5
The Darkroom

From the very beginning of archaeological photography it has been the usual practice to develop black and white films on location, whenever possible; and at once to see if the record has detailed exactly what was wanted before further digging, which may bring destruction, is resumed, or if it shows precisely how an object or whatever is found in relation to its surroundings before it is extricated. However, in more recent years differing attitudes have developed among directors and photographers concerning the best time to process pictures – whether they should be processed as soon as they are taken, no matter what the time, or in bulk following the day's work. Perhaps the type and amount of work will dictate the method, and it might vary considerably. In fact some excavation locations may make it advisable not to process film at all on location. Obviously the developing and printing of pictures in bulk is a tremendous time saver and even a saving of materials. It also can be argued that if photographers in other kinds of work had to hold up progress while they ran and developed a negative, chaos would result. One might reasonably say that a wedding photographer can't easily do it over, nor can a pilot engaged in mapping while flying over enemy territory. Moreover it might rightly be assumed that if the photographer does not have enough confidence in either his skill or his equipment to do it right in the first place, he is maybe not so skillful or the equipment is inadequate. Perhaps archaeological photographers have been overcautious in wanting to see their results immediately, and there may have been a good deal more excuse for this in the past when exposures were largely a matter of guesswork and experience. Some photographers must have spent half of their time traveling back and forth between site and darkroom to the point where today this seems a bit ridiculous. With modern equipment this press to see the almost instant results appears quite unnecessary, though with Polaroid it is certainly possible. Still many photographers using traditional methods and materials will yet maintain the need for immediate examination of negatives, most likely because they have been committed to ways of working they have developed over the years. Undoubtedly the problem is one not so much of not trusting themselves, but of a realization of the hazards of processing in hot solutions or other

difficult conditions, and there is surely some justification for such a viewpoint if this is the reason.

Two possibilities could make much of this whole section superfluous: 1. the use of Polaroid films only and/or 35-mm color transparencies from which black and white prints could be made later; and 2. the lack of proper facilities for a darkroom or lack of electricity for printing. However, most photographers, for the present at least, are likely to follow the more standard practices and require a darkroom; but on the other hand if the film size is 4 × 5 in. or smaller, a change bag and a daylight developing tank is entirely feasible, and the printing can be done later.

SETTING UP THE DARKROOM

Noted in previous chapters was the admonition to simplify things as much as possible through choosing the fewest types of items that will adequately suffice. Even in a commercial darkroom one of the most persistent problems is the storing of items for easy availability and yet preventing the room from becoming a cluttered jumble like the proverbial drugstore or five and dime store window. When the latter situation develops efficiency inevitably drops, contamination usually occurs, and mistakes are made which result in frequent and costly wastage. The darkroom must be both *simplified* and *organized*; this cannot be stressed too strongly.

But first let us start with the location of the darkroom. Concurrent with early attitudes toward the photographer were similar feelings toward his darkroom – any unwanted cubbyhole had to do. With later appreciation of the value of photography came the realization by site directors that better darkrooms meant better photographs, and as a result the darkroom now has a top priority in room location, often even more thought being given to it in this regard than to the office.

Since traditionally the first important assignment for the photographer upon arrival is the securing and setting up of the darkroom, he needs to give it immediate attention (even if the site is an old one, the darkroom will still require cleaning and arranging). Many factors must be weighed carefully in making a wise selection of the room. It must be easily accessible of course, yet not in such a prominent place as to be an open invitation for every curious individual that happens by. The room should be adequately large and hopefully capable of being ventilated in some way while still maintaining darkness. And in hot and/or humid weather

the interior cubage needs to be somewhat larger than that which elsewhere would be considered satisfactory (perspiration dripping on prints or negatives can be disastrous indeed). Naturally the choice should be governed in part by the availability of water. Almost never is the photographer at a site lucky enough to have running tap water for use; it usually has to be carried into the darkroom in sizable containers from the outside. The darkroom therefore should be reasonably near the outside water source when possible. In hot and/or humid climates the room should be on the side of a building (if any) away from the sun and under trees (if any). In past sites use has been made of tents, caves, and other unlikely places, and they undoubtedly will serve again in the future. Further, the darkroom should have electrical outlets, or at the very least a power line from the generator or other source of electricity.

And it hardly needs saying that it is not a darkroom if it cannot be darkened! The method of making a selected room lighttight is first to place opaque black paper over all window panes with masking tape. Windows should not be closed permanently, for it is not impossible that in hot weather some work could be done at night with the windows partly opened for better ventilation (if no moonlight or other outside lights interfere). After the windows have been blacked out the room is then tested for light leaks, this being done at the brightest hour of the day and after one's eyes have adjusted to the darkness of the interior. Where chinks of light appear the place is marked with a piece of chalk and that area is later covered with more opaque paper. Such a procedure will probably need several testings to make sure no light filters in, and time spent in this way will offer obvious rewards later in trouble-free processing and in unfogged pictures. Doors often give more trouble with light leaks than do windows, as at least one door will have to be used for entering and leaving. If there is a light bulb outside the door, make sure it is burning for the test. Some kind of weather-stripping might well be packed with the camera supplies for the purpose of sealing off door or window leaks. A black cloth that can be rolled up and down is a general practice. Special care is required for stopping light entering around or through the ventilating system, whatever this may be.

The most practical kind of ventilating system that will provide adequate air circulation is a double fan blower, such as can be purchased at photo stores, and can be screwed on to the door or on a wood panel in place of a window pane. One fan is for drawing air in and the other for blowing it out. The room also needs to be dustproof – really almost an impossibility, but it can be made to keep out most lint-type dust

even though dust from a duststorm will permeate the tightest of rooms.

Then some method of insuring privacy while at work is necessary. Sometimes signs do not serve very well, but they should be available nevertheless to put up on the door. Two signs ought to be made (in your language and possibly also in the local native one): the first, a permanently attached one, might read 'Unauthorized Personnel Keep Out'; the second, a temporary and reversible one, could read on one side 'Photo Darkroom IN USE – Do Not Enter' and the other side 'Photo Darkroom Not In Use'.

Once all of the foregoing is done attention can be given to outfitting the room with workbenches and shelves. Considerable horizontal surface space is needed within the room, so table-high working areas could well stretch around most of the entire inner circumference. Shelves for storage of various supplies are desirable – almost essential – and they should keep the supplies from becoming contaminated and in the way. If the working surfaces are smooth and can be kept reasonably clean, fine, but the chances are that the use of shelving or wrapping paper or cheap, thin plastic will be necessary, particularly in the sections where loading of films and handling of the printing papers is done.

Speaking of sections, Cookson notes [55] the need for division of the room into two quite separate parts: the dry section and the wet section. Experienced darkroom workers do this instinctively – probably have even from the beginning – but it is well to make a point of it and warn against violating this principle (see fig. 24). Nothing can be more aggravating or disastrous than drippings from drying films or developing

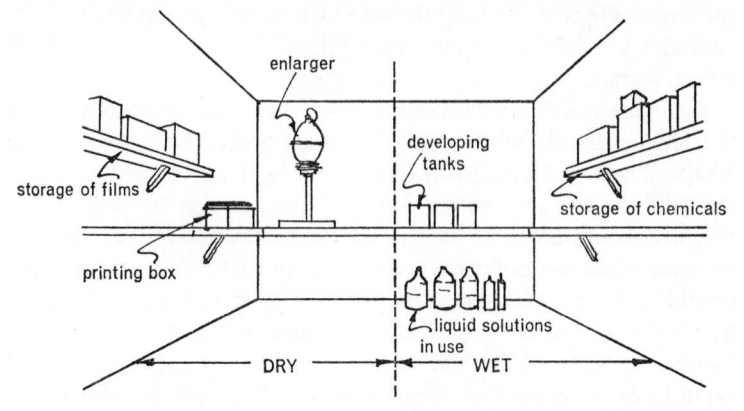

Figure 24.   Possible arrangement of site darkroom showing dry and wet halves

tanks getting on dry films or printing papers. These two sections need not be equal in size, the dry area being used exclusively for operations like loading and unloading sheet film holders or your own 35-mm cassettes, for printing and enlarging; while the wet side is used for other activities connected with developing, fixing, and washing of films and prints. In both areas should be kept towels, the rough absorbent type like huckaback, attached to a clip of some sort. Certainly before handling dry films or papers the hands must be completely free of perspiration or working liquid solutions. Moreover there should be a systematic direction of movement during successive steps of the work – right to left or vice versa, it doesn't matter. But this further helps to organize the room into an efficient working place.

It is possible to make use of the darkroom for drying films and prints (the latter are often best dried on frames of cheesecloth netting in an open cabinet), but another location where there is better circulation of air to dry them more rapidly may be available. This area should also be a place where dust will not settle on the surfaces of the materials. Extreme care needs to be exercised to prevent people from handling or even touching the drying materials, for like a freshly painted park bench few individuals can resist the impulse to test for themselves. In the event that the darkroom must be used for drying purposes one or more simple but open cabinets for prints can be placed under the shelves or tables, and a wire or string stretched across the middle of the room separating the dry and wet areas. From the latter, films on clips or in their developing holders can be hung. Picture-frame wire is a good choice, being strong, flexible, non-rusting (for a season), and unsagging. But make sure that you hang the wire high enough that you don't hang yourself! The bottoms of the hanging films should clear your head by several inches.

Safelights as well as a white inspection light should be positioned over the developing area, whether the developing process be by tank or tray. The wall color is unimportant, except that light colors will help reflect the safelight and give better vision. Camera equipment, except film holders, should never be kept in the darkroom because of moisture; however, since the darkroom is theoretically cooler than any other, or should be (in hot climates), bulk films can be stored in it and thus be handy for loading in total darkness. Films and printing papers on shelves should be set on their edges rather than left flat to prevent any possible stress marks that could occur if left in that position over a lengthy period of time.

It is entirely probable that some sites may offer only battery power for electricity – there will be no power lines or generator. In this case things like ventilators are out – short of rigging up a windmill – as are enlargers and printing boxes. One would have to rely upon a printing frame and a battery lamp (it's been done!). If one suspects or knows there is a lack of electricity or knows that it might be unreliable, it would be wise to seriously consider using only Polaroid films or transparencies – or, as mentioned earlier, a trained photographer should be able to judge a negative of fair size as to its quality and contents.

One good procedure is to note the temperature in the darkroom at various times of the day (and night) to find out when is best for working there. Another recommended procedure is never to mix developer or hypo solutions in the darkroom itself, but in a suitable adjacent area. This means such an area also should have ready access to water and be out of direct sunlight.

DEVELOPING

The basic methods and step-by-step processing are not discussed here, for this information, as was said at the beginning of the book, is readily available in many excellent publications, and photographers who contemplate archaeological work will need to know these thoroughly or already do. However, certain tips or suggestions may prove valuable in the field, particularly those that pertain to working under adverse conditions or those that may readily be overlooked.

Manufacturers recommend certain dependable developers for specific films, and often supply these developers with chemicals already mixed and packaged. It is advisable to follow these recommendations, and further to purchase the chemicals in a ready-mixed form that is not liquid, since it is not the chemicals but water weight that is paid for when shipping them. Almost no one today bothers to weigh out chemicals and mix any of the standard formulas themselves, for there is little savings in cost and the manufacturers can do it more accurately and with less danger of contamination. But some special formulas, not necessarily developing formulas, may be needed, so conversion tables are included in Appendix B (p. 124). The usual procedure is to mix a batch, say a gallon, and keep it in a tightly stoppered bottle or jug when not in use. Because partly filled bottles contain a fair amount of air, which acts to reduce the life of the solution, a good practice is to use several small

bottles for stock solutions – *well labeled!* The life of the developer also will be determined by a number of other factors, such as the number and size of films or papers processed in it; how much of its surface is exposed to air and for how long during developing; whether the use is intermittent or continuous; the room temperature; and so forth. The use of a replenisher is suggested as a means of economy and extended life. Incidentally chemicals not in use ought to be kept high and dry on shelves.

Simple but necessary are stirring rods. Solutions should be mixed somewhere other than the darkroom (a repeat because of its importance), and keeping the working solutions at the desired temperature can be the most difficult of all problems in many places, especially in hot and tropical areas. A handy conversion table of Fahrenheit to Centigrade is also found in Appendix B (p. 126). And of course a reliable darkroom thermometer is required. Chemicals dissolve in hot water better, so some form of heating unit may be desirable, though possibly the kitchen stove (if any) would work admirably. To store the solutions a cool place is beneficial for their long life, but cool places are sometimes hard to come by. Perhaps there is a large walk-in refrigerator available in the kitchen – a bit of wishful thinking! Any kind of small refrigerator is good for temporarily cooling down a bottle of solution, but if space is at a premium for food, such a procedure might be frowned upon. Another answer is the use of desert bags, canvas bags that keep contents cool by a method of evaporation. This method is usable for water, but hardly for chemical solutions, since the chemicals will increase in strength as the water part of the solution evaporates. If one uses this technique for cooling water, the bags should be hung in the shade and where there is the best chance for a draught or breeze. These bags will drip until fully saturated. Another possibility, but not a very satisfactory solution in really hot places, is to dig a pit in the ground and insulate the top. Such a pit would probably need to be at least 5 ft deep; and it would not cool down things in the tropics, merely keep them from getting too warm. Still another answer, and this, too, merely provides a keeping place, is to cover with a wet rag the outside of a jug as it sits in the shade and a draught – the same principle as the desert bag – though the rag has to be kept moist. It does have the advantage of keeping the solution itself from evaporating.

Ice is seldom available in areas where it might be needed, except possibly ice cubes from a refrigerator. In the latter case they can be used in a tray of water, and the developing tank or tray allowed to rest in that.

Or some have used ice in a glass set in the developing tank to cool the surrounding solution. The process of cooling by the agency of melting ice is improved by adding salt to the ice.

At the other extreme it may be necessary to keep a solution from getting too cool, in which case an immersion heater, like those presently on the market for heating water in a cup for brewing a cup of coffee or tea, would be inserted in the solution for long enough to raise the temperature to the necessary level. Or the developing tank could be set in a tray where the latter has the immersion heater in it. Since metal trays or tanks conduct heat or cold more rapidly, hard rubber or plastic ones may be more desirable in extremes of temperature.

All kinds of water may have to be used, some containing unwanted ingredients. Distilled water is the best for mixing stock solutions of developers, as it has negligible amounts of impurities or none, but it would be available only in rare instances for the archaeological photographer. Drinking water is the next best, and even this may have in it some unwanted impurities. There are several methods of treating water so that it can be used for photographic purposes. To coagulate slime and colloidal organic matter, mix 15 grains of potassium alum in 1 gallon of water, and the resulting sludge can be removed by filtering the solution through a finely woven piece of cotton or linen cloth, while the small amount of alum has no harmful effect in developing or fixing baths. To remove calcium and magnesium salts, as well as coagulating slime, use 3.34 oz of sodium oxalate to 1 quart of water. Hypo (fixing) and washing waters do not require the purity of developers. It is even possible to wash films and papers in seawater for the most part if they are finally rinsed in fresh water. Also a hypo clearing agent cuts down tremendously on washing time.

Through the recommended developing temperature is 65°F (18°C) or 68°F (20°C) most developers can be used up to 75°F (24°C) by adjusting the development time (see instruction sheets with films or on cans in which chemicals are packaged). Charts of developing times and temperatures are also printed for most films in a useful, but comparatively expensive book, the *Photo-Lab-Index*, published by Morgan and Morgan, Hastings-on-Hudson, New York. This book, which can be kept up to date by purchasing quarterly supplements, has much valuable technical material in it that can be of considerable value to the photographer. There are two possibilities for high temperature developing that can make the difference between a constant headache and relatively trouble-free developing. One is the use of certain chemical additions to

regular developers to make it possible for development up to 95°F (35°C), and the other is to use tropical developing solutions made specifically for the purpose. The first mentioned possibility is simply the addition of sodium sulfate (desiccated), and recommended amounts and temperatures are given in Appendix B for Kodak films (p. 127).

The second method for hot climate development is the use of Kodak DK-15 Tropical Developer or DK-15a Low Contrast Tropical Developer, each of which allow for development up to 90°F (32°C).

Both methods require rinsing in a tropical hardener solution after development and before fixing (see Appendix B, p. 127). Stop bath is a must between all developing and fixing, else the fixer will wear out too rapidly.

Whether one uses tanks or trays for developing and fixing is a matter of preference. Tanks are more economical in terms of both chemicals and water when more than several sheets of film are being done, and certainly if a roll of film is being processed. Tanks more easily combat the dust problem than do trays, a factor well worth considering in areas subject to much dust – like most sites! In any case tanks and trays should be labeled so that they are always used for the same purpose and not mixed (the exception is daylight developing tanks into which all solutions are poured). Enameled trays are discouraged, for they chip too easily.

One-shot developing solutions are commercially available in standard formulas, but are quite uneconomical for archaeological site work unless very few films are to be developed. Naturally the developing time will vary according to the usual factors such as temperature and freshness of solutions, but also according to desire, that is, whether one wants a contrasty or flat negative, in which case there can be over- or under-development. Two pictures on the same type of film taken under the same conditions may require different densities, depending upon the subject matter. Alison Frantz, writing about a general view as compared to a close-up of a potsherd half-buried in the earth, points this out as she says, 'if negatives of these two subjects are processed in exactly the same way and the outdoor scene appears with a full gradation of tones, the potsherd will resemble a mid-turtle camouflaged on a mud bank. If the turtle is brought to life, the other picture will be nothing but a harsh admixture of chalky highlights and coal-black shadows.'[56] When available light conditions force the shooting by underexposure, this can be partly compensated for by forcing development and pulling the negatives when they are at the point of best compromise between density

and fog due to the forcing. Reduction or intensification by chemical means had best be left for later work at home base.

Some photographers like to be able to visually inspect their pan films more than is normally allowed by the dark green safelight. This can be accomplished by desensitizing the films before development in a solution of desensitizer (available commercially). After half development the films can be pulled out for inspection at 1-minute intervals for as long as 10 seconds under a yellow-green safelight.

If you are developing Panatomic-X films where strobe has been used, it is recommended that you extend the time of development by 15 per cent. Other pan films may be processed normally.

Safelights should be kept 4 ft from the sensitive materials during processing. For pan films the safelight filter for regular developing should be a Wratten Series 3 (dark green) with a 15-watt bulb which is used for a few seconds only after development is half completed. Printing and enlarging papers like Velox and Kodabromide require a Wratten Series OA (yellow-green). Orthochromatic films need a red filter.

Two clocks are helpful in the darkroom. Set the hands of the second clock (not running) to the time you want to stop developing, and you will not need to trust to memory, for time can become a confusing element when you are doing many things in the darkroom. The second clock can be a broken one – or even just a face with hands.

An inexpensive fixing test solution is made by mixing 1 oz of potassium iodine in 16 oz of water, and a drop of it produces cloudy-white precipitate in an exhausted fixer; it does not affect the bath otherwise. Often not enough water is available for the proper washing of all the fixer out of the films, so they may have to be rewashed and refixed at a later time. Photo-Flo or other wetting agent added to the last rinse will prevent streaking of negatives.

Not really a part of darkroom procedure, but some information that could be very useful, is the method of making a ground-glass substitute. The ingredients are 200 cc of water, 20 grams of rice starch, and 100 cc of water-glass (sodium silicate sol, sp.g. 1.3). The solution is made by mixing the rice starch with the water, then adding the water-glass. The mixture is poured over a piece of clear glass that has been leveled and then allowed to dry. The surface is easily scratched, but can be protected with a cellulose lacquer.

PRINTING AND ENLARGING

The sizes of films used will determine the need for a printer or enlarger, for smaller negatives (probably less than 4 × 5 in.) need to be blown up with an enlarger. Chemically the procedures are the same, and they are similar to those used in processing negatives, the main difference being that another developing formula is employed. Printing or enlarging in the field is usually confined to proofs, the final glossy prints being made back at home base where time and control are more favorable. So it is the negatives that are all-important and to which most care is devoted.

One solution to not having to stock many grades of enlarging papers is to use a variable contrast type, the density of which is altered by the proper filters on the enlarger. Problems revolving about the possible lack of electricity for this operation were discussed earlier, and nothing need be added here, except that in an emergency sunlight could be used in the printing frame by directing the light through a trapdoor improvised in a window of the darkroom. It hardly needs pointing out that there are many difficulties with the procedure, if indeed it can be done satisfactorily at all.

As to the equipment the only additional things necessary are a good small enlarger (if enlargements are needed) or printing box or frame (if no enlargements are desired) and either a timer or stopwatch to gauge the exposures. The kind of enlarger is largely a matter of personal choice, but it must have a good lens. Smallness is desirable only as a matter of packing. Needless to say it should be a stable one. A paper cutter might be handy if the film size warrants, though scissors are really adequate for proof prints.

MARKING AND FILING OF NEGATIVES AND PRINTS

Larger negatives can be fully annotated on the margins (see fig. 25), but this is not possible with miniatures, for the sprocket holes occupy too great a portion of the edges, though a name and number could be put on the latter, one letter or digit between each sprocket hole (see fig. 26).

Negatives 2¼ in. square or larger should be kept singly in separate envelopes of the glassine variety, a semitransparent paper which allows one to view them through the envelope and thus not risk getting fingerprints all over their surfaces. Miniature films can be cut in strips of three

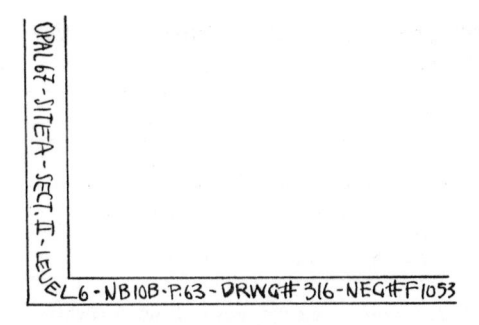

Figure 25. Marginal notations for large negatives
Note: these can be put on either adjoining or opposite margins, whichever are widest.

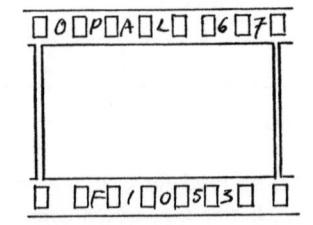

Figure 26. Marginal notations for miniature negatives

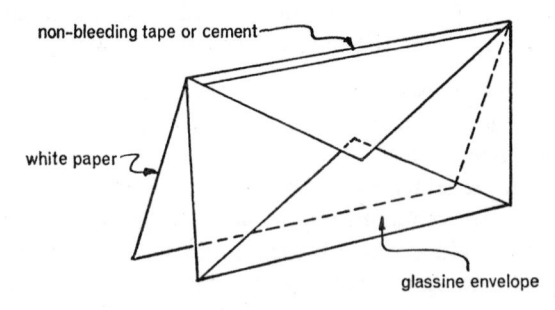

Figure 27. Method of attaching paper to glassine envelope (scratched on with a pin point for opaque edges).

or four frames, whatever the envelope size permits. In any case information corresponding to the photographer's notebooks needs to be entered on the envelope. Since the slick surface of the glassine paper is not conducive to legible writing, a piece of white paper should be attached (see fig. 27), and another chart printed on it, again by means of a rubber

stamp or mimeographing (see figs. 28 and 29). Negatives should then be filed by sequence in a suitable container having a lid to keep out the dust.

location	OPAL		date	1967
site	A	sect. II	level	6
n.b.	10B		page	63
drwg. #	316		neg. #	F 1053

Figure 28. Chart for negative envelopes in F series (field)

location	OPAL	date	1967
object	COIN	#	1734
		neg. #	5165

Figure 29. Chart for negative envelopes in S series (studio)

While Indian ink can be used for marking on negatives it tends to crawl on the surface. A better ink, which dries rapidly and does not spread or flake off, can be made from the following solutions:

Solution A: 10 grams of feric chloride and 25 cc of acetone.
Solution B: 15 grams of tannic acid and 75 cc of acetone.

Mix the two solutions as needed; use a clean steel penpoint and make sure the latter is tight in the holder, else it will easily pull out when the pen is wiped free of ink.

Black and white prints from negatives can be filed together in sequence according to negative number in any suitable container with a lid.

If black and white Polaroid is used, prints should be given the same number as the negatives of the 55 P/N film, the negatives and prints filed in the same manner as above. When color Polaroid prints are obtained they should be put in separate envelopes, each of which should be annotated like regular negatives.

Negatives should be brought back personally by the photographer and, if he is conscientious, he will not let them out of his sight, not even trust them to a porter, but rather carry them in a brief case by hand and guard them with extreme watchfulness, for they represent the season's work and are irreplaceable; lose them and the whole season's efforts by the entire team is lost except for any objects that may have been found.

Chapter 6
Back at Home Base

Following the season's work at the dig, there will be much to do upon return to the home base, for the photographer's job is then possibly only half done – if that! There will be more photographing, printing of negatives, filing, taking care of equipment, preparing lecture slides and perhaps movies, probably preparing lectures themselves, and may be even publication efforts.

The budget for home base operations is normally part of a total budget, as is that for the field operations. In any case there are films, papers, and expendables to be included on the budget for this work too, the one major difference from field work being that, if the photographer runs short of any materials, rectification is easily achieved by a quick trip to a photographic supply store.

Many of the following steps discussed will undoubtedly proceed concurrently, but they have been separated here for simplicity in presentation.

EQUIPMENT

The temptation after unpacking might be to get at the work of making prints or viewing the processed color slides (and movies) returned by mail, but it is imperative that the equipment be properly cared for at once. It represents a considerable sum of money and must be thoroughly cleaned by the photographer and those few items not to be used until the next season must be put away in good condition. A major portion of things however will be needed during the next phase of the operation, the preparing of final prints.

Cameras in particular should be minutely inspected, their interiors cleaned of any dust and checked for corrosion; telescopic tripod legs and sockets should be lubricated with powdered graphite; studio lamps replaced if they have burned many hours (they turn darkish at the top); and the files checked to see if negatives have begun to deteriorate in any way. When there has been a water shortage at the site and the washing of negatives minimal, they should be rewashed and refixed immediately.

Unused films will probably be needed shortly, so they should be stored temporarily in a cool place.

MORE PHOTOGRAPHING

The opportunity to do some really fine photography under controlled conditions now awaits the photographer, for small finds (sometimes big ones) that have been brought back will need to be photographed or rephotographed under more ample lighting, particularly those that have been cleaned, repaired, or restored – a procedure that goes on throughout the full year, for this is a very lengthy task. Besides these items there may be site plans and drawings to photograph for publication (if they are not already done). Certainly there will be special groupings of finds needed for publication, and here the director will work closely with the photographer to get exactly what is desired.

Basically the same set-up as described in Chapter 3 is used for photography at home base, but with more refinements. Just as for most photography, there is the same need for a studio and darkroom, for light control, etc. New or clean backgrounds need to be on hand and probably a greater variety of them can be pressed into service, especially for color work.

PRINTS

Since only proof prints are usually made in the field, a complete set(s) of 8 × 10-in. (or at least 5 × 7-in.) glossies will probably be wanted, possibly not of all negatives, depending upon the number of similar shots of any one subject, but a substantial amount. The director should go over all of the proof prints and check those which he feels are likely to be wanted for publication or other use. Some of the negatives will surely need to be blown up to a large size for exhibition purposes, these being on a matte surface rather than glossy paper. Prints for publication are normally made at least one-quarter larger than the final cut to allow for cropping and reduction, and single weight paper is satisfactory for these glossies.

It is possible that certain arrows or annotations may have to be added to prints, though it is often said that photos needing such markings are bad ones. Nevertheless there can be special reasons for requiring such

notations. The marking should be done with a watercolor opaque pigment or show-card tempera applied by a pen, and both paints will need to be slightly diluted with ammoniated water to which is added a few drops of liquid mucilage (shake well!). This should take to the surface of the print, but in the event that it does not adhere evenly or spreads, a non-crawl solution can be obtained at an art store. For an eraser a twirl of absorbent cotton on a round toothpick dipped in water will do nicely. However, the best efforts at this kind of marking are amateurish. A more professional method is to make blow-ups of the material needing annotating, and to do lettering on the large print, which is then rephotographed to produce a negative with better looking notation on it. Modern lettering on acetate sheets that is easily affixed to the surface of the prints is a most satisfactory way of achieving the desired results.

NEGATIVE FILING

New negatives of items just taken are added to the original file, but with a special designation letter (such as B for Base) preceding the registry number. Another notebook similar to the one used in the site studio is advisable.

A procedure that will involve considerable time at the beginning, but which will save endless hours of hunting through the negative file later, is the making of a 3 × 5-in. card file for each negative, cross-indexed by groupings of subjects, such as general views, sections, trenches or pits, walls, wall paintings, mosaics, sculpture, pottery, jewelry, small finds, and miscellaneous. On the basic card for each negative carrying the registry number space is left for recording from time to time where and when the negative is used for publication, slides, or exhibition purposes.

SLIDES

Hopefully transparencies, either negative or positive, were taken in the field of the many phases of the dig and of finds. As was indicated earlier in this book, 2 × 2-in. color slides are the generally preferred size today – and in color if possible. When positive transparencies are shot there is little to do further except mount them between cover glass and label them. This includes any necessary masking off of undesirable areas, an

aspect often overlooked or neglected – to the detriment of a projected presentation. If the transparencies were taken on negative film such as Kodacolor, positives will need to be made of them unless this was originally stipulated in the processing instructions to the lab. When duplicates are required the use of original negative color film is the more satisfactory system, for duplicates from positives leave much to be desired. Either process probably can be best done by Kodak or other commercial labs, for they can use special duplicating techniques of preflashing the film. The Kodak pamphlet *Producing Slides and Film-strips* (Publication No. S-8) is recommended reading if you want to try your own duplicating.

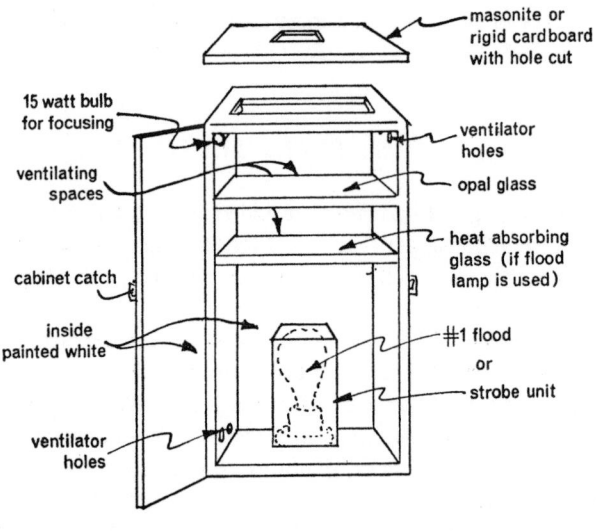

Figure 30.   Light box for copying films or slides

When transparencies are wanted from black and white negatives, the easiest procedure is to rephotograph the negatives on more negative film (pan type). This involves the copying technique described in Chapter 3, except that an enclosed light box is necessary, either to contain a No. 1 flood lamp or a small strobe unit (see fig. 30). Small weights may be needed to hold the film material flat on the top of the box.

It is possible that larger color negatives have been used and 2 × 2s wanted of them, in which case the same system is employed, only that a color negative is inserted in the copying camera.

MOTION PICTURES

If by any chance movies were made on location, the resulting film will need to be screened, cut, spliced, have sound added, and duplicate prints made. The last two items will probably need to be done commercially. For all these procedures the photographer, unless already familiar with their intricacies, should consult available general books and pamphlets on the subject, as well as the more specialized ones like *Basic Titling and Animation* by Kodak (Publication No. S-21) and *Magnetic Sound Recording* also by Kodak (Publication No. P-26).

Appendix A
Check Lists of Supplies and Equipment

Obviously not all of the following items will be required, depending upon certain equipment situations or objectives.

FOR OUTDOOR PHOTOGRAPHY AT THE SITE

main field camera and normal lens
  wide-angle lens
  telephoto lens
filters
  A (red)
  B (green)
  C5 (blue)
  G (orange)
  K2 (yellow)
  neutral density # 1
  + 1 lens
  + 2 lens
  + 3 lens
  − 1 lens
filter holders
filter adapter rings
filter retaining rings
filter cases
sunshade
film holders
accessory back for roll films
accessory back for Polaroid films
spare ground-glass for camera back
cable release
focusing cloth and clip
carrying case
lens brush
lens tissue

bubble level
main tripod and universal head
light tripod and universal head
films
  sheet
    pan
    color
    Polacolor
    Polaroid
    infrared
  roll
    pan
    color
    Polacolor
    Polaroid
  miniature
    pan
    color
    Polacolor
    infrared
  movie
supplemental field camera and
  normal lens
  wide-angle lens
  telephoto lens
carrying case
adapter backs
movie camera

carrying case
exposure meter (reflection-type)
exposure meter (incident-type)
ballpoint pens and refills
field notebooks
spiral-bound notebooks
field scales and sheaths
chalkboard or signboard
  letters
aluminum ladder
garden spray for wetting sections
strobe unit and battery
  battery charger
  slave units
  spare batteries
flash gun and batteries
flash bulbs
synchronizing cords to cameras
portable flood (for movies) and
  charger
reflectors
field kit

Plasticine or 'Silly Putty'
1-in. paint brushes
2-in. paint brushes
#6 camel hair brushes
small whisk broom
small trowel
small dustpan
tablespoons
flat-bladed table knife
kitchen paring knife
penknife
white chalk
roll of white tape
roll of white chalk line
plumb bob and line
small scissors
small-scale sticks
metal tape measure
handfull of 10 penny nails
tape recorder
  tape
  spare batteries

FOR PHOTOGRAPHY AT THE SITE STUDIO

main studio camera and normal
  lens
miniature or roll camera for
  records
  normal lens
  telephoto lens
filters
  (same as for outdoor)
  X-1 (light green)
  polarizing
filter adapter rings
films
  pan

  ortho
  color
  copying
  movie
studio tripod and universal head
cable release
camera stand for verticals
studio lamps (3,200°K) and sockets
  reflectors
  spare bulbs
spot lights in housings or
  spot lamps in reflectors
  spare bulbs

lamp, spot, and reflector stands
  clamps
metal stands for vases
power extension cords
double sockets
polarizing screens for studio lamps
neutral gray test card
light box with ground-glass or opal
  glass top and extra glass
paper backgrounds (cardboard)
  white bristol board or card-
    board
  black (smooth or veloured)
  colors (for color work)
fabric backgrounds
  black velveteen
  colors (for color work)
exposure meter (reflection-type)
exposure meter (incident-type)
color meter
Plasticine or 'Silly Putty'
chalk
matting spray
liner
lampblack paste
table scale sticks
large sheets of tracing paper for
  diffused light (rolled in tube)

FOR THE FIELD DARKROOM

opaque black paper (for making
  room lighttight)
masking tape
weather stripping
rolls of black cloth
shelving paper or plastic
double fan ventilator
huckaback towels and clips
nails for building shelves
power extension cords
enlarger
print box or frame
safelight and bulbs
safelight filters (Series 3, OA)
white inspection light
thermometer
2 clocks (one not working)
stopwatch
tanks or trays
stirring rods
print tongs
immersion heater
primus stove and fuel
picture wire for hanging films
printing papers (for proofs)
enlarging papers (for proofs)
developing chemicals (films)
developing chemicals (papers)
stop bath chemicals
fixing chemicals (films and papers)
clearing chemicals
water-purifying chemicals
wetting agents
fixing test chemicals
tropical chemicals
gallon jugs/bottles (tight stopped)
desert bags
graduates
funnel
cheesecloth netting
weighing scales
film clips

MISCELLANEOUS

glassine negative envelopes
file box
packing lists
plastic bags
change bag (for daylight loading)
silica gel
moistureproof tins for films
ventilated cabinet (for hot climates)
ultraviolet lamps

glycerin
shaving mirrors
close-up calculator
aerial photo calculator
fill-in flash calculator
microscope attachment
bellows for miniature camera
Indian ink or substitute and pens
aspirin!

Appendix B
Tables and Charts

CONVERSION TABLE: U.S. CUSTOMARY TO METRIC LENGTH

Yards (yd)	Feet (ft)	Inches (in.)	Millimeters (mm)	Meters (m)
1	3	36	914.4	0.0194
0.333	1	12	304.8	0.3048
0.0277	0.0833	1	25.4	0.0254
0.00109	0.00328	0.03937	1	0.001
1.0936	3.2808	39.37	1000	1

CONVERSION TABLE: CENTIMETERS TO INCHES AND INCHES TO CENTIMETERS

Centi-meters	Milli-meters	Inches (approx.)	Inches	Centi-meters	Milli-meters
1	10	0.39	1	2.54	25.40
2	20	0.79	2	5.08	50.80
3	30	1.18	3	7.62	76.20
4	40	1.57	4	10.16	101.60
5	50	1.97	5	12.70	127.00
6	60	2.36	6	15.24	152.40
7	70	2.76	7	17.78	177.80
8	80	3.15	8	20.32	203.20
9	90	3.54	9	22.86	228.60
10	100	3.94	10	25.40	254.00

CONVERSION TABLE: FEET TO METERS AND METERS TO FEET

Feet	Meters	Meters	Feet	Inches (approx.)
1	0.30	0.25		10
1½	0.45	0.50		20
2	0.61	0.75		29
2½	0.76	1	3	3
3	0.91	1.25	4	1
3½	1.07	1.50	4	11
4	1.22	1.75	5	9
5	1.52	2	6	7
6	1.83	2.5	8	2
7	2.13	3	9	10
8	2.44	4	13	1
9	2.74	5	16	5
10	3.05	6	19	8
12	3.66	7	23	
15	4.57	8	26	3
20	6.10	9	29	6
25	7.62	10	32	10
30	9.14	12	39	5
40	12.19	15	49	3
50	15.24	20	65	7
75	22.86	25	82	
100	30.48	30	98	5
150	45.72	40	131	3
200	60.96	50	164	

CONVERSION TABLE: AVOIRDUPOIS TO METRIC WEIGHT

Pounds (lb)	Ounces (oz)	Grains (grain)	Grams (g)	Kilograms (kg)
1	16	7000	453.6	0.4536
0.0625	1	437.5	28.35	0.02835
		1	0.6648	
	0.03527	15.43	1	0.001
2.205	35.27	15430	1000	1

CONVERSION TABLE: U.S. CUSTOMARY LIQUID TO METRIC MEASURE

Gallons (gal)	Quarts (qt)	Fl. ounces (fl oz)	Cubic centimeters (cc)	Liters (liter)
1	4	128	3785	3.785
0.25	1	32	946.3	0.9463
		1	29.57	0.02957
		0.03381	1	0.001
0.2642	1.057	33.81	1000	1

CONVERSION TABLE: BRITISH LIQUID TO U.S. LIQUID

British liquid	U.S. liquid
1 fl oz	0.96 fl oz
1 pt (20 fl oz)	19.2 fl oz = 1 pt (16 fl oz)
1 qt (40 fl oz)	38.4 fl oz = 1 qt (32 fl oz)
1 gal (160 fl oz)	153.7 fl oz = 1 gal (128 fl oz)

Note: oz per British imperial qt × 0.8 = oz per U.S. qt
oz per British imperial qt × 25 = cc per liter
cc per liter × 0.3999 = oz per British imperial qt

CONVERSION TABLE: CUBIC INCHES TO CUBIC CENTIMETERS

Cubic inches	Cubic centimeters	Cubic inches	Cubic centimeters
1	16.387	8	131.10
2	32.774	9	147.48
3	49.161	10	163.87
4	65.548	20	327.74
5	81.936	30	491.61
6	98.323	40	655.48
7	114.71	50	819.36

CONVERSION TABLE: FLUID OUNCES TO CUBIC CENTIMETERS AND CUBIC CENTIMETERS TO FLUID OUNCES

Fluid ounces	Cubic centimeters	Cubic centimeters	Fluid ounces
1	30	50	1.69
2	60	75	2.54
3	89	100	3.38
4	119	150	5.07
5	148	175	5.92
6	178	200	6.76
7	207	225	7.61
8	237	250	8.45
9	267	300	10.14
10	296	350	11.83
11	326	400	13.52
12	355	450	15.21
13	384	500	16.91
14	414	750	25.36
15	444	900	30.43
16	474	1,000	33.81
24	710	2,000	67.63
32	946	3,000	101.44
64	1,892	4,000	135.26
128	3,785	5,000	169.07

CONVERSION TABLE: FAHRENHEIT TO CENTIGRADE

°F	°C	°F	°C
50	10	73	22.78
59	15	74	23.33
68	20	75	23.89
69	20.55	77	25
70	21.11	86	30
71	21.67	95	35
72	22.22	104	40

USE OF SODIUM SULFATE (DESICCATED)
FOR TROPICAL DEVELOPING

Developers	Temperature	Per quart	Per liter
D-11 & D-76 (films)	75°–80°F (24°–27°C)	1 oz 290 grains	50 grams
	80°–85°F (27°–29.5°C)	2½ oz	75 grams
	85°–90°F (29.5°–32°C)	3 oz 145 grains	100 grams
D-72 (papers)	75°–80°F (24°–27°C)	3 oz 145 grains	100 grams
	80°–85°F (27°–29.5°C)	4 oz 75 grains	125 grams
	85°–90°F (29.5°–32°C)	5 oz	150 grams

Note: if it is necessary to develop at 90°–95°F, decrease the time about ¼.

STOP BATH OF TROPICAL HARDENER FOR USE
BETWEEN DEVELOPING AND FIXING

Between 68° and 80°F (20° and 27°C)			Between 80° and 95°F (27° and 35°C)		
water	32 oz	1 liter	water	32 oz	1 liter
acetic acid (28%)	1 oz	32 cc	potassium		
sodium sulfate			chrome alum	1 oz	30 grams
(desiccated)	1½ oz	45 grams	sodium sulfate		
			(desiccated)	2 oz	60 grams

Note: these solutions also come prepared commercially.

Appendix C
Notes on the Plates

Plates 1–9 were photographed at Aphrodisias, which is being excavated by a New York University team of archaeologists under the direction of Kenin Erim.

1. General view of ruins at Aphrodisias in process of reconstruction and showing such details as binding on column drums, the assemblage of probable parts into groups, and the separating out of pieces of different age (note twisted columns of later than Greek origin in foreground). The lighting is from the ten-o'clock position providing fine detail with shadow contrast that obscures exceptionally little. Only top faces of a few column pieces in foreground wash out under very bright sun. (35 mm.)

2. Medium close view of Corinthian and Ionic temples, in nearby area to subject of Plate 1, give a good record of both column and capital details. Again lighting is high so that shadows delineate but do not obscure. (35 mm.)

3. Well-cleaned excavation in which different layers of various temples are visible, including octagonal pavement blocks of one level. Shadows are strong but detail is fairly easily seen in them, because the light, surrounding areas are reflecting some sunlight into the darker portions. Supplemental flash or strobe could have improved the shadow area. (35 mm.)

4. Again excellently cleaned areas with sharp edges and brushed stones. However, note the higher light that produced less shadows and allows for very nice textural detail of wall facing. (35 mm.)

5. Archaeologist and local helper taking measurements at Aphrodisias, the latter man using a scale stick divided in half-meter sections. Both persons in themselves provide a scale for the ruins and neither stare at the camera but are engaged in actual work. (35 mm.)

6. Two native workmen are observed as involved in repairing some step-seats of a theater, with tools, braces, cement, and other important aspects of the work evident in the picture. Though the background is in shadow (which silhouettes the workers) there is still enough detail to see an inlaid pattern of the stone paving. (35 mm.)

7. The best use of sunlight to bring out most sculptural details of this capital is shown here. A high sun slightly to the side is effectively employed. (35 mm.)

8. Incised lettering is in effect a textural detail to be emphasized, and to be shown adequately the light must be across the face of the stone rather than directly at it. The resulting sidelighting on the lettering makes it clearly readable, even if it is much smaller than actual size. The inscription is a later Christian addition to the original Greek temple at Aphrodisias. (35 mm.)

9. Use of strobe to illuminate an ancient underground aqueduct brings out the textural detail, especially along the left wall and slightly vaulted ceiling. The strobe unit was held away from the camera to the left and above. (35 mm.)

10. Inca bundle containing a gold figurine from Peru against a lighted ground-glass. The exposure is shorter than for the photograph opposite, which makes the subject darker, and at the same time emphasizes the textural qualities.

11. The same object on a black background. Note that the tapestry material has to be made light to contrast with the surrounding area, and this decreases the textural detail.

12. Well-cleaned skeleton of a Pueblo Indian from the excavations at Pueblo San Cristobal, New Mexico. Size of the whisk indicates the skeleton was an adult. See how the earth has been removed from under the bones as far as practicable to allow for shadows that make them clearly visible against the only slighter darker mud floor.

13. The lighting upon this $46 \times 18\frac{1}{2}$-in. brocaded cotton and wool double shirt from Peru is from both left and right. This can easily be seen by noting the shadows at the sides. While the pattern is clear, the texture is minimized.

14. Observe the lighting used in this 9½-in. long double pottery bowl from Grenada, Nicaragua. It is lighted directionally from nearly straight above. Detail around the neck, like that around the base, is diminished because of the heavy shadow. While some light is reflected upward from the underneath table surface, none illuminates the very lowest portions. However, it should be noted that the detail of the texture and incised lines around the bulge is excellent.

15. Here the light is from the right front and not as harsh, for additional diffused light was reflected onto the bowl from the left. While texture and linear detail is perhaps not as good on the mid-sections, the overall effect is much better. In both instances the difference in background has little effect upon the bowls, except that the dark upper area in Plate 14 tends to balance the heavy shadow under the bowl.

16. With this unfinished tapestry sampler from Peru, not only the pattern is pronounced but also the texture is accentuated, for observe the single shadow under the tie cords. The lighting was from the left to emphasize the horizontal warp threads.

Credits: Photos 1–9 by William R. Simmons, New York University Photographic Services; photos 10–16 through the courtesy of the American Museum of Natural History, New York.

References

1. M. B. COOKSON, *Photography for Archaeologists*, London, Max Parrish, 1954.
2. 'Truth Before Beauty or, the Incompleat Photographer', *Archaeology*, Vol. III, No. 4 (winter), 1950, p. 202.
3. *loc. cit.*
4. *The Seven Caves*, New York, Knopf: London, Cape, 1957, p. 338.
5. P. C. HAMMOND, *Archaeological Techniques for Amateurs*, New York, Van Nostrand, 1963, p. 94.
6. ROLAND WELLS ROBBINS and EVAN JONES, *Hidden America*, New York, Knopf, 1959, p. 264.
7. R. J. C. ATKINSON, *Field Archaeology*, London, Methuen, 1946, p. 157.
8. 'Truth Before Beauty or, the Incompleat Photographer', p. 204.
9. ROBBINS, *op. cit.*, p. 220.
10. *ibid.*, p. 219.
11. PAUL JOHNSTONE, *Buried Treasure*, London, Phoenix House, 1957, p. 9.
12. *ibid.*, p. 44.
13. ROBBINS, *op. cit.*, p. 218.
14. ATKINSON, *op. cit.*, p. 163.
15. *loc. cit.*
16. M. WHEELER, *Archaeology from the Earth*, Oxford, Clarendon Press, 1955, p. 174.
17. ATKINSON, *op. cit.*, p. 163.
18. WHEELER, *op. cit.*, p. 175.
19. DOUGLAS OSBORNE, 'Solving the Riddles of Wetherill Mesa', *National Geographic*, Vol. 125, No. 2 (February 1964), p. 186.
20. *Art and Archaeology*, Englewood Cliffs, N.J., Prentice-Hall, 1963, p. 52.
21. *loc. cit.*
22. *loc. cit.*
23. 'Truth Before Beauty or, the Incompleat Photographer', p. 203.
24. *ibid.*, p. 209.
25. J. S. ACKERMAN and R. CARPENTER, *Art and Archaeology*, p. 54.
26. *Copying Techniques*, Boston, Mass., American Photography Pub. Co., 1940, pp. 114–16.
27. ACKERMAN and CARPENTER, *op. cit.*, p. 37.
28. L. COTTRELL (ed.), *The Concise Encyclopedia of Archaeology*, New York, Hawthorne Books, 1960, p. 71.

29. R. F. HEIZER, 'Archaeological Investigations at the Mouth of the Amazon', Smithsonian Institution, Bureau of American Ethnology, Washington, D.C., 1957, *Bulletin*, 167, p. 7.
30. G. R. WILLEY, 'Prehistoric Settlement Patterns in the Virú Valley, Peru', Smithsonian Institution, Bureau of American Ethnology, Washington, D.C., 1953, *Bulletin*, 153, p. 3.
31. ATKINSON, *Field Archaeology*, Plate II.
32. *ibid.*, Plate III.
33. COTTRELL, *op. cit.*, p. 71.
34. ACKERMAN and CARPENTER, *op. cit.*, p. 24.
35. *loc. cit.*
36. *ibid.*, p. 26.
37. Volume 20, Number 1 (January 1967), pp. 67–8.
38. Volume 19, Number 4 (October 1966), pp. 273–6.
39. *Under the Mediterranean*, Englewood Cliffs, N.J., Prentice-Hall, 1963, p. xi.
40. 'Underwater Archaeology: Key to History's Warehouse', *National Geographic*, Vol. 123 (1963), No. 1, p. 142.
41. *Under the Mediterranean*, p. xii.
42. *loc. cit.*
43. *loc. cit.*
44. *ibid.*, p. 191.
45. CAPTAIN JACQUES-YVES COUSTEAU, 'Fish Men Discover a 2,200-Year-Old-Greek Ship', *National Geographic*, Vol. 105 (1954), No. 1, pp. 1–36.
46. GEORGE F. BASS and PETER THROCKMORTON, 'Excavating a Bronze Age Shipwreck', *Archaeology*, Vol. 14, No. 2 (summer), 1961, pp. 78–87.
47. PETER THROCKMORTON, 'Oldest Known Shipwreck Yields Bronze Age Cargo', *National Geographic*, Vol. 121 (1962), No. 5, pp. 697–711.
48. GEORGE F. BASS, 'Underwater Archaeology: Key to History's Warehouse', *National Geographic*, Vol. 123 (1963), No. 1, pp. 138–56.
49. *ibid.*, p. 143.
50. 'Use of Infrared Photography in Archaeological Work', *American Antiquity*, Salt Lake City, Vol. 20 (1954), p. 84.
51. P. C. HAMMOND, *Archaeological Techniques for Amateurs*, p. 151.
52. *ibid.*, p. 152.
53. DON BROTHWELL and ERIC HIGGS (eds.), *Science in Archaeology*, London, Thames and Hudson, 1963, p. 595.
54. *loc. cit.*
55. M. B. COOKSON, *Photography for Archaeologists*, pp. 80–2.
56. 'Truth Before Beauty or, the Incompleat Photographer', p. 213.

Bibliography

The following books and periodicals deal with photography to some extent, but the only major book on the subject is Cookson.

ACKERMAN, JAMES S. and CARPENTER, RHYS, *Art and Archaeology*, Englewood Cliffs, N.J. and London, Prentice-Hall, 1963, p. 241.

ATKINSON, R. J. E., *Field Archaeology*, London, Methuen, 1946, p. 238.

BASS, GEORGE, *Archaeology Under Water*, New York, Praeger: London, Thames and Hudson 'Ancient People and Places' series, 1966.

BEUTTNER-JANNAECH, JOHN, 'Use of Infrared Photography in Archaeological Field Work', *American Antiquity*, Salt Lake City, Vol. 20 (1954), pp. 84–7.

BROTHWELL, DON and HIGGS, ERIC (eds.), *Science in Archaeology*, London, Thames and Hudson, 1963, p. 595.

COLTON, HAROLD S., *Field Methods in Archaeology*, New York, Flagstaff, 1952.

COOKSON, MAURICE BRUCE, *Photograph for Archaeologists*, London, Max Parrish, 1954, p. 123.

COTTRELL, LEONARD (ed.), *The Concise Encyclopedia of Archaeology*, New York, Hawthorne Books: London, Hutchinson 'New Horizon' series, 1960, p. 512.

CROSS, E. R., *Underwater Photography and Television*, New York, Exposition Press, 1954, p. 258.

CROY, O. R., *Camera Close Up*, New York and London, The Focal Press, 1961, p. 240.

DÉRIBERÉ, M. J. PERCHEZ and TENDRON, G., *La Photographie Scientifique*, Paris, Paul Montel Publications, 1951, p. 127.

FRANTZ, ALISON, 'Truth Before Beauty or, the Incompleat Photographer', *Archaeology*, Vol. III, No. 4 (winter), 1950, pp. 202–14.

FRAPRIE, FRANK R. and MORRIS, ROBERT H., *Copying Techniques*, Boston, Mass., American Photography Pub. Co., 1940, p. 128.

FROST, HONOR, *Under the Mediterranean*, Englewood Cliffs, N.J., Prentice-Hall: London, Routledge, 1963, p. 278.

HAMMOND, PHILIP C., *Archaeological Techniques for Amateurs*, New York and London, Van Nostrand, 1963, p. 329.

HEIZER, ROBERT FLEMING, *A Guide to Archaeological Field Methods*, Palo Alto, California, The National Press, 1959, p. 162.

KENYON, KATHLEEN MARY, *Beginnings in Archaeology*, New York, Praeger: London, Phoenix House, 1953, p. 228.

Bibliography

LAHEE, FREDERIC H., *Field Geology*, New York and London, McGraw-Hill, 1952, p. 883.

LUNIAK, BRUNO, *The Identification of Textile Fibres*, London, Pitman, 1953, p. 177.

MILLER, WILLIAM C., 'Uses of Aerial Photography in Archaeological Field Work', *American Antiquity*, Salt Lake City, Vol. 23 (1957), pp. 46–62.

SHAW, LESLIE, *Architectural Photography*, London, Newnes, 1949, p. 192.

TAYLLOR, JOAN DU PLAT, *Marine Archaeology*, London, Hutchinson, 1965, p. 208.

WHEELER, SIR MORTIMER, *Archaeology from the Earth*, Oxford, Clarendon Press, 1955, p. 221.

The following Kodak pamphlets mentioned in the text are recommended.

Aerial Exposure Computer, Publication No. R-10.
Basic Titling and Animation, Publication No. S-21.
Master Photoguide, Publication No. R-21.
Magnetic Sound Recording, Publication No. P-26.
Notes on Tropical Photography, Publication No. C-24.
Photography through the Microscope, Publication No. P-2.
Producing Slides and Filmstrips, Publication No. S-8.
Studio Lighting for Product Photography, Publication No. O-16.
Techniques of Microphotography, Publication No. P-52.
Ultraviolet and Infrared Photography, Publication No. M-3.

Index

Figures in italics refer to the photographic plates.

Contents

Preface

This book was written principally for 1. the professional photographer entering or interested in entering the archaeological field; 2. the professional archaeologist desiring to acquaint himself more completely with the work of the photographer who may be with him, or with advances in this specific area of activity; 3. the amateur photographer wanting to know about archaeological aspects of photography; 4. the amateur archaeologist who has decided to do a bit of the photographing for himself, but needs some additional photographic information not found in the usual books on photography; 5. the student who may become either an archaeologist or archaeological photographer; and 6. the advanced history of art student who may more fully appreciate archaeology and archaeological photography after learning something of its complexities, problems, and possibilities.

By no means is the book intended to present those elementary photographic facts known to any photographer (even most amateur ones) as may be found in the many good publications on photographic methods and materials readily available at libraries and bookstores. Such factual information, while perhaps new to the non-photographer, would not materially assist in his understanding the special requirements of archaeological photography, nor is there a need for such information for the person already knowledgeable in basic photography. What the book does, for the most part, is point to photographic equipment and materials that can or should be selected and indicate methods of working with them, hopefully for the purpose of making the life of the archaeological photographer a bit less harrowing on the one hand, and to open up further directions in understanding for non-photographers on the other.

The author wishes to acknowledge the ever present encouragement of his friend and colleague, Professor Henry C. Atyeo, and the additional friends too numerous to list by name. He would also like to express his gratitude to archaeologist James R. McCredie of the Institute of Fine Arts, New York University, for his many helpful suggestions upon reading the first draft of the manuscript. Certain pictures included were taken by William R. Simmons of New York University's Photographic Services and others by staff members of the American Museum of Natural History. Thanks are hereby given for permission to use these.

HAROLD C. SIMMONS
New York City, Summer 1967

Printed in Great Britain by
Richard Clay (The Chaucer Press) Ltd, Bungay, Suffolk

Archaeological Photography

HAROLD C. SIMMONS

New York: NEW YORK UNIVERSITY PRESS
London: UNIVERSITY OF LONDON PRESS LTD
1969